STEFAN GATES
SCIENCE
YOU CAN
EAT

DK | Penguin
Random
House

Written by Stefan Gates
Senior Editor James Mitchem
US Editor Mindy Fichter
US Senior Editor Shannon Beatty
Project Art Editor Charlotte Bull
Designed by Eleanor Bates, Rachael Hare,
Karen Hood, Sadie Thomas
Edited by Clare Lloyd
Photographer Lol Johnson
Jacket Designer Elle Ward
Jacket Coordinator Issy Walsh
Additional illustrations by Kitty Glavin
Managing Editor Penny Smith
Managing Art Editor Mabel Chan
Senior Pre-Producer Nikoleta Parasaki
Producer John Casey
Creative Director Helen Senior
Publishing Director Sarah Larter

First American Edition, 2019
Published in the United States by DK Publishing
1450 Broadway, Suite 801, New York, NY 10018

Text copyright © Stefan Gates 2019
Copyright © 2019 Dorling Kindersley Limited
DK, a Division of Penguin Random House LLC
19 20 21 22 23 10 9 8 7 6 5 4 3 2 1
001–305906–June/2019

A catalog record for this book
is available from the Library of Congress.
ISBN 978-1-4654-6843-7

DK books are available at special discounts when
purchased in bulk for sales promotions, premiums,
fund-raising, or educational use. For details, contact:
DK Publishing Special Markets, 1450 Broadway,
Suite 801, New York, NY 10018
SpecialSales@dk.com

Printed and bound in China

A WORLD OF IDEAS:
SEE ALL THERE IS TO KNOW

www.dk.com

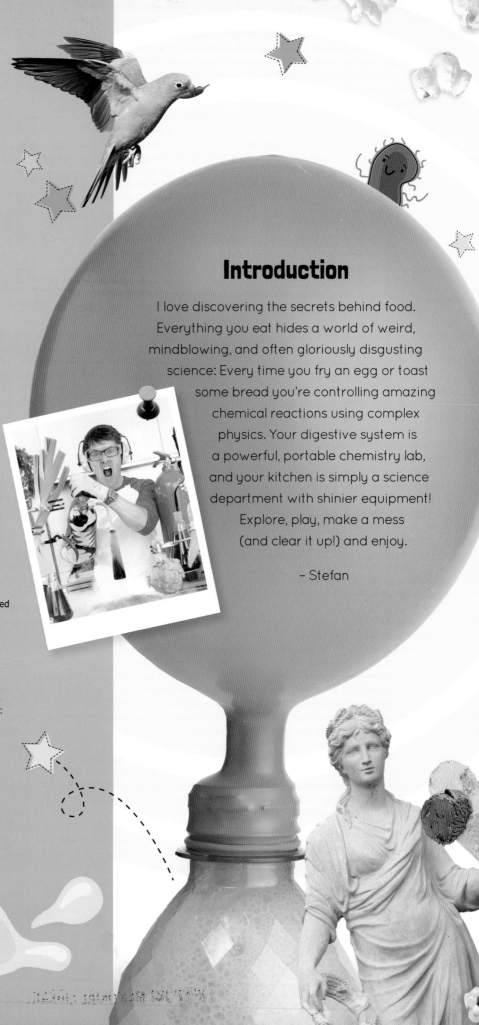

Introduction

I love discovering the secrets behind food.
Everything you eat hides a world of weird,
mindblowing, and often gloriously disgusting
science: Every time you fry an egg or toast
some bread you're controlling amazing
chemical reactions using complex
physics. Your digestive system is
a powerful, portable chemistry lab,
and your kitchen is simply a science
department with shinier equipment!
Explore, play, make a mess
(and clear it up!) and enjoy.

– Stefan

STEFAN GATES

SCIENCE
YOU CAN
EAT

DK

FREEPORT MEMORIAL LIBRARY

CONTENTS

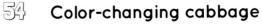

WHERE IT ALL STARTS

We love food for its flavor, but **the main reason** we need to eat is because food gives us energy. That energy originates from plants—but how does that energy get into the plants in the first place? It's because of an amazing process called **photosynthesis** that almost all life on Earth depends on for fuel. Photosynthesis also takes carbon dioxide from the atmosphere and creates oxygen from it—the same oxygen we breathe. It's safe to say we owe a LOT to photosynthesis.

A chemical in plant leaves called chlorophyll (which is what makes them green) absorbs energy from the sun and uses it to power the photosynthesis reactions.

How it works

In a chemical reaction **powered by sunlight**, plants absorb carbon dioxide and water, and transform them into glucose and oxygen. Plants use some of the glucose for energy and store any extra as starch and oils. When we eat the plants (or animals that have eaten the plants), this stored chemical energy can be converted into energy that our bodies can use.

Carbon dioxide

Carbon dioxide is absorbed from the air through holes called stomata on the underside of leaves.

Close-up of stomata

Water and minerals from the soil are absorbed through the plant's roots and travel through the rest of the plant, including the leaves.

Water and minerals

6

Oxygen

The sun

Seasonal science

If plants need to absorb sunlight to create energy, why do so many of them drop their leaves in winter? Well, winter months have less sunlight so plants **can't photosynthesize efficiently** so they go to sleep for the winter. They then drop their leaves so that high winds don't damage the tree structure.

The leaves go brown in winter as the tree re-absorbs chlorophyll from its leaves and stores it for use next summer.

See it happen

You can actually watch photosynthesis happening by using a piece of pond weed called **Elodea Canadensis** (often found in pet shops). Cut around ³/₄in (2cm) off the top of a piece of the weed, and attach a binder clip to one end to weigh it down. Lower the weed into a tall glass so it's completely underwater, then point a light at it. Within a minute or so you should see little bubbles forming and escaping from the cut. That's oxygen. The weed is absorbing carbon dioxide from the water and using it to photosynthesize.

Bubbles

It's not the most amazing sight, but it's pretty cool to be able to see the most important chemical process in the entire world!

Photosynthesis provides food for nearly all living things. Without it, life on Earth would stop.

WHAT IS FOOD?

A healthy adult eats around a ton of food every year, so it might sound odd to ask "What is food?" But even the simplest-looking egg, steak, or lettuce is fantastically complex and contains many chemicals. **The idea of eating chemicals may sound strange and unnatural,** but nothing could be further from the truth: Everything from food, phones, cars, shoes, fingers, brains—and your entire body—is made from chemicals held together in various combinations.

Water

We get a surprising amount of the water our bodies need from our food. There's a huge amount of water in many foods, even if we think of them as dry. **Cheddar cheese** is 37 percent water, and **lettuce** is 95 percent.

What makes up our food?

Macronutrients
These provide energy. There are three types: fats, carbohydrates, and proteins.

Micronutrients
We only need tiny amounts of these but they are essential for life. They're called vitamins and minerals.

Fiber
Very important for gut health.

Water
Often a major component of any food, and vital for life.

Non-nutrients
Pretty much everything else such as smell and taste compounds, colors, waxes, emulsifiers, acids, preservatives, gels, gases, and sweeteners. These may be important to cooks and eaters, but are not essential to life.

Fiber

Dietary fiber is anything that can't be broken down by our bodies' enzymes (chemicals found in our saliva, stomach, and small intestine that break down large complex molecules into smaller, simpler ones). **Vegetables, beans, and grains** contain a lot of fiber. It's very important for our digestive health to eat plenty of it.

Milk is a great source of the micronutrient calcium. It's vital for healthy teeth and bones.

Food and health

The definition of food is "any nutritious substance that people or animals eat or drink, or that plants absorb in order to maintain life and growth." All of these substances are essential for our survival, and without them our organs would begin to fail. But eating too much fat or sugar can also lead to health problems. It's best to eat a **balanced diet** and lead an active lifestyle.

Protein

Essential for building muscle, bones, and tissue, as well as repairing damaged cells and building new ones. Adults need around 2oz (60g) of protein every day. It's found in **meat, fish, eggs, dairy products, beans, peas, lentils, nuts, and seeds**.

Carbohydrates

Carbohydrates are our main source of energy and they come in different forms. The simplest ones are sugars, and the more complex ones are starches. These include **beans, pasta, and bread**. During digestion we break down complex carbohydrates into simpler sugars that our bodies can use for energy.

Fat

Fats are essential to life and often contain essential micronutrients. There are two main types of fats: saturated fats, which are usually solid at room temperature (found in **cheese, butter, and meat**), and unsaturated fats, which are usually liquid at room temperature (found in **olive oil and avocados**).

Taste with your tongue

Taste receptors

Nerve fibers

Your tongue is covered in tiny bumps containing taste buds that detect flavors. Children have around 10,000 taste buds, adults only have around 6,000.

Sweet

Sugars taste wonderfully sweet, and we are hard-wired to enjoy this sensation from the time we are born. It's because of evolution: Sweet foods contain a high amount of energy, so our ancestors were more likely to survive if they ate sugary foods.

TASTE

Your tongue is AMAZING! It's vital for your enjoyment of food, and is packed with receptors that analyze taste and texture and pass the information to your brain. But despite how clever it is, your tongue can only tell the difference between **five main tastes**: sweet, salty, savory, bitter, and sour.

Salty

We think of salt as something we sprinkle on food to enhance flavor, but plenty of foods such as soy sauce, many cheeses, and seaweed have a strong salty taste. Salt is essential for our bodies, but too much of it is bad for our health.

There are very tiny traces of poisonous cyanide in fruit seeds such as apple pips.

Bitter

Our taste receptors are very sensitive to bitter food and most people find it unpleasant. Even so, bitter drinks such as coffee are enjoyed around the world, and vegetables such as Brussels sprouts have a trace of bitterness, too.

People who have an unusually high sensitivity to tastes are called supertasters. To them, bitter food tastes extra bitter and sweet food can taste extra sweet. Maybe you're one of them!

Our dislike of bitter foods probably developed to help our ancestors survive: many poisons taste bitter.

Sour

The sensation of sourness comes from acidic foods such as lemons, oranges, tomatoes, and vinegars. Most fruit is slightly acidic, and the acid helps to slow down rotting. We tend to like sourness when combined with sweetness.

Savory

Also known as "umami," which is a Japanese word for "pleasant savory taste," savory foods contain rich, deep flavors, and are found everywhere from mushrooms, to cheese, meat, and roasted tomatoes.

Taste is complicated, and although scientists know that different tastes interact with our receptors, there's still a lot of work to be done to find out exactly how.

TRICK YOUR TASTE BUDS

This fun trick proves that flavor is hugely influenced by **senses other than taste**, and that our sense of **sight alone** can fool us. Don't let people see you set up the trick—it may affect the results.

Add 1 pint (600ml) water, 6 tsp sugar, 2 tsp lemon juice, and 4–6 drops of food coloring to a jug. Stir to dissolve the sugar.

2

3 Repeat this process with different food coloring, making jugs with 6 tsp sugar and 2 tsp lemon juice in each. Pour into glasses until each person has a rainbow of five different colored drinks.

Pour equal amounts into four glasses so you have four identical-looking colored drinks.

You will need

- Water
- Sugar
- 3–4 lemons, juiced
- Red, orange, yellow, blue, and green food coloring
- Large jug
- Spoon
- 20 small glasses or cups
- Paper and pens

These amounts are for four people, but you can scale the recipe up or down so more or fewer people can take part.

Why this works

Our brain begins to form an expectation of flavor as soon as we see food or a drink, way before we've even tasted it. This expectation can be enough to transform our actual experience, and can make us think that identical-tasting drinks taste different just because they are different colors.

4 Copy the chart below onto paper and give each of your four friends a copy. Tell them to taste each drink and mark an "X" in the box to show what they think is the flavor of each drink.

5 Compare the answers and see if your friends made choices based on the color of the drinks. They will almost certainly have strong opinions about what the drinks are, even though the drinks all taste exactly the same!

WHAT FLAVOURS ARE THE DRINKS?

Put an "X" in the box that matches the flavor to the color

	Lemon	Strawberry	Blueberry	Apple	Orange
Red drink					
Orange drink					
Yellow drink					
Blue drink					
Green drink					

This trick may not work on all your friends—some of them may figure it out! If they do, congratulate them on their sense of taste!

HOW SMELL WORKS

Smells plays a huge role in how much we enjoy our food. But what are they? Smells come from flavor volatiles (molecules that evaporate easily so they can move through the air). These are breathed in through the nose and reach **chemoreceptors** in the **olfactory bulb**, a part of the nervous system located behind our eyes. These receptors transmit information about smells to the brain.

Olfactory bulb

Chemoreceptors

Flavor volatiles

Our sense of smell is very personal. Some people really like smells that other people can't stand!

A lot to learn

There's a lot we don't know about how smells work and how flavor volatiles and chemoreceptors interact. But we do know the flavor volatiles we breathe in get dissolved in a sticky mucus in our noses, and are detected by our chemical sensors—though the method of detection is still a **little bit of a mystery.** However, we do know the information is sent to our brains as tiny electrical signals.

Our mucus is constantly flowing, and is entirely replaced every ten minutes. This is why you can smell one substance, followed by another one soon after.

Types of smells

Some experts think smells can be roughly split into **different categories**. And it's useful to group smell types together so we can communicate what we are experiencing. Here's a simple categorization of ten groups.

Fragrant
(flowers and perfumes)

Sweet
(chocolate, toffee, and vanilla)

Woody
(fresh-cut grass and pine)

Chemical
(cleaning products)

Fruit
(any non-citrus fruity smell)

Minty
(eucalyptus and mints)

Toasted and nutty
(popcorn, almonds, and peanut butter)

Citrus
(oranges, lemons, and limes)

Decayed
(rotten meat, eggs, and sour milk)

Pungent
(smoke and blue cheese)

Whenever you're eating, why not give your food a good sniff and see if you can detect any of the categories above?

Genetic differences can have an impact on our sense of smell. About 2 percent of people are thought to be insensitive to sweaty body odor!

THE WORLD'S SMELLIEST FRUIT

This huge, spiky beast is known as the "King of Fruits" in Southeast Asia, and opinion is divided on whether it tastes wonderful or awful. **Durians** are so smelly they are banned from many public spaces across Thailand and it's illegal to carry them on public transportation in Singapore. But many people love the taste, and durians fetch a high price in markets across the world.

What do they smell like?

The smell of a durian is a complex mixture of flowers, rotten onions, sweaty underwear, gas, custard, rotten egg, cheese, and—there's no nice way to say this—poop. In chemistry terms, the substances that create these smells are rotten-smelling fatty acids and sulfur-based compounds.

What do they taste like?

Although many people regard durians as revolting, plenty of people love their smell and taste, and describe them as rich, custardy, creamy, sweet, and almondy. The less ripe the fruit is, the more mild and delicate the flavor.

Husk

Pulpy cell

Inside the fruit

Inside the tough, spiky husk there are five pulpy cells, each containing three seeds. The pulp is the most commonly eaten part but the seeds can also be eaten roasted, fried, or boiled. The seeds are poisonous to humans if eaten uncooked since they are packed with toxic fatty acids. But orangutans are immune to the poison and have been seen feasting on the seeds.

A durian growing

There are several species of durians, but the most common is *Durio zibethinus*. They are pollinated by bats, which are drawn to the sweet nectar that drips from the fruit.

Durian trees are massive, and the fruit themselves can be the size of footballs, weighing up to 8lb (4kg).

Sight

The sight of food can change your enjoyment of it **long before it reaches your mouth.** Blood flow to the brain dramatically increases when a hungry person sees pictures of food. But if food doesn't look familiar, such as pasta dyed blue or potatoes dyed green, you're less likely to enjoy it—even if it tastes and smells the same.

Research shows that even plates affect our enjoyment of food. Both small and red plates make us eat less, and if red coloring is added to a drink, we think it tastes sweeter!

WHY WE LOVE FOOD

The taste of food on your tongue is just one of many sensations that combine in your brain to create the overall sense of its **flavor.** Smell, sight, touch, sound, heat, and even pain, memory, the color and size of your plate, and your mood are just as important.

Touch

Your mouth is packed with receptors that **collect information about your food** and send it to be processed by your brain. Thermoreceptors tell you how hot or cold food is, and other receptors analyze texture such as shape, sliminess, and how hard or soft food is. All of this makes a difference to how we enjoy what we eat.

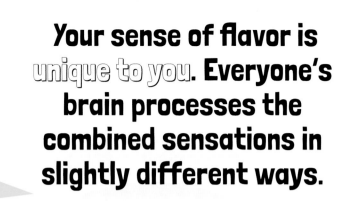

Your sense of flavor is unique to you. Everyone's brain processes the combined sensations in slightly different ways.

Sound

You'd think that sound wouldn't affect flavor, but crunching sounds from chips or raw carrots make us think they are **fresher**, so we enjoy them more. One reason chips are packed in foil bags is to enhance this sensation even more. Also, the sound of a soft drink fizzing in the glass is known to make you enjoy it more.

Multisensory grub

Chocolate is a great example of a food that **triggers multiple senses**. It's sweet, has a complex smell, and it gives amazing touch sensations in our mouths because of how it melts. As it melts, touch receptors on our tongue send our brains a pleasurable sensation, and because you remember having enjoyed chocolate from the last time you tasted it, your brain is primed to enjoy it again. It's like turbo-charging your senses!

Researchers from Oxford University in England found that Italian opera music made people enjoy Italian food even more.

SALT AND OTHER MARVELOUS MINERALS

Salt can be easy to overlook, but it's incredible stuff. It's the most important **flavor enhancer** we have, and adding a little to our food can really make it come alive. Salt is essential to our bodies—if we didn't eat enough we wouldn't be able to live However, eating **too much salt** can be bad for you.

The chemistry of salt

Salt is a mineral, which means it's a naturally occurring chemical compound that's not produced by life forms such as plants or animals. However, minerals are often found in plants and animals—having originally come from soil. A lot of different chemicals are classified as salts, but the one we eat is almost always **sodium chloride**.

It can be hard to know how much salt we eat because it's added to a lot of foods by manufacturers.

Why do we need it?

Salt is an essential tool for our central nervous system, which uses the sodium in salt to **transmit electric signals** through our cells and to our brain (yes, you are electric!). You have around 7oz (200g) of salt in your body, and there's a complex system that regulates your salt-to-water balance—mostly through the production of sweat and urine.

Salt was very valuable in ancient times. Roman soldiers were given a salt allowance. The word "salary" comes from the Latin "salarium" (salt money).

Preserving food

For thousands of years, salt has been one of the most important tools for preserving food. **Bacteria can't survive in salty environments**, so fish (especially cod) used to be salted and dried so it lasted months instead of days. Meat, such as bacon, is also salted (for both flavor and preservation), and pickling mixtures are often made of salt, sugar, vinegar, and water.

Pickling recipe:

Salt + **Sugar** + **Vinegar** + **Water**

What else is salt used for?

Around 200 million tons of salt are produced each year, but only a **little of that is used for food**. The majority is used to produce chemicals. Salt is also used for water softening, farming, and a surprising amount is spread on roads during cold weather to stop ice from forming.

Marvelous minerals

We have traces of a lot of minerals in our bodies, but the five that are essential to life are calcium, phosphorous, potassium, sodium, and magnesium. Calcium is the most abundant—adults' bodies contain up to 2¼lb (1kg) of calcium in their bones and teeth. Minerals are found in food, as well as in other objects we don't eat.

Calcium
Found in milk.

Phosphorus
Found in matches.

Potassium
Found in soap.

Sodium
Found in salt.

Magnesium
Found in fireworks.

Purple

The rich purple color of beets comes from something called **betanidin**. It breaks down when exposed to light, heat, and oxygen—none of which are found in your intestines—so it survives your digestive system pretty much intact. Because of this, it turns your poop a deep red color when it's excreted.

FOOD AND COLOR

The natural color in our food is made by substances called pigments, most of which come from a set of closely related chemicals. Color can be added to food to make it look more appealing, more healthy, more fun, or even to hide rotten food. These colors can be **artificial or natural**.

Nettles

Alfalfa

Green

The most well-known food pigment is **chlorophyll**, the natural green substance found in many plants. It can be extracted from nettles, grass, and alfalfa to create an intense green color to add to food. If you ever see the ingredient E140 on a label—that's chlorophyll.

Red

Tomatoes start off green but as they ripen, a chemical called **lycopene** makes them turn red. This helps the plants reproduce, because unlike green pigments, orange, yellow, and red pigments attract pollinating insects.

Beetle juice

E120 is a deep red color made from crushed cochineal beetles. The beetles live on cacti, mainly in Peru, and when crushed, create a rich red color. This is refined and used as a food additive. Why? So that food companies can write "No artificial colors" on the packaging!

You'd have to eat around five carrots a day for at least a month to start to see the effects.

Orange

Carrots contain something called **alpha- and beta-carotene**. If you eat a lot of carrots on a regular basis you can suffer from carotenosis, which can turn your skin orange! It's most common in babies that eat a lot of pureed carrots, but it's harmless and easily reversed.

Blue foods aren't very appealing, and studies have shown that they can reduce our appetites.

Spirulina

Coal

Artificial colors

Artificial colors are mostly made from a coal extract. They are bright, bold colors and are cheap to produce, but some people are worried that they can cause hyperactivity in children. Food additives are given **E numbers**, and are strictly regulated when used in food, but before laws came in to protect the public, people were often poisoned by careless food producers. Highly toxic red lead and vermillion were once used to color cheese and children's candy.

Blue

There are hardly any blue foods, with the exception of blueberries, blue corn, blue cheese such as Stilton, and some lobsters (before they are cooked, after which they turn pink!). A natural blue food dye can be made from an algae called **spirulina**.

WAYS OF COOKING

There are four **reasons** we cook food—to make it taste better, to make it safer by killing bacteria in it, to make it more digestible, and to preserve it or stop it from rotting. But as for **ways** to cook food? There are a lot of options.

Roasting

Dry heat from the circulation of hot air in an enclosed space, usually an oven, is called roasting. This creates indirect transfer of heat, and is great for large dishes such as root vegetables or cuts of meat. Baking is similar to roasting, but refers to making bread, pastries, cakes and other flour-based foods. These need even heat to cook properly.

Frying

Food is fried by heating it to a very high temperature with a fat such as butter or oil, either in a frying pan (shallow frying) or in a deep pot (deep frying). Frying is great for thinner pieces of meat and vegetables because the high temperatures cause reactions that create wonderful flavors.

Frying temperatures can be terrifyingly hot, and people need to take great care not to burn food or cause an accident.

All the heat comes from the bottom of the pan, so food needs to be flipped.

Modern ovens have fans to help the air (and heat) circulate better.

The oil or butter helps transfer heat to the food more evenly.

"Sous vide" (French for "under vacuum") is a precise cooking method where food is vacuum-packed and cooked very gently for a long time in water that's hot but well below boiling point.

Maillard reaction

The amazing smell of baking bread and the magically meaty flavor of a grilled steak are due to the **Maillard reaction**. It's a series of chemical reactions that happen at high temperatures and create a huge range of complex smells and flavors.

Boiling

This is the method of submerging food in water that has been heated until it begins to turn to steam, which at sea level is 212°F (100°C). Pasta, potatoes, and vegetables are often boiled. Poaching is a gentler variation where the water is kept below boiling point, but is still hot enough to cook the food.

Barbecuing

Barbecued food is cooked over charcoal or wood. It can be cooked quickly at high temperatures over direct heat, but usually it's cooked slowly over indirect heat, often with the addition of wood chips to add smoky flavors. The smokiness that comes from burning wood or coals gives the food a really wonderful flavor.

Heat is transferred through the water into the food from all around.

It's easy to control the temperature of the water.

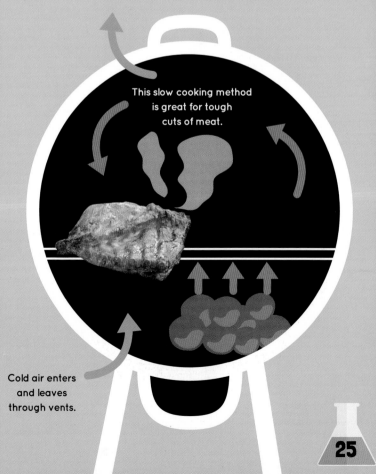

This slow cooking method is great for tough cuts of meat.

Cold air enters and leaves through vents.

MICROWAVES

Microwave ovens use some amazing physics to cook your food. Unlike regular ovens that cook by circulating hot air, microwave ovens blast your food with **radio waves**. This method of cooking is very fast—around six times faster than a normal oven—making microwave ovens very energy efficient. The downside is they can't heat food above the boiling temperature of water, so they'll never brown a steak!

The walls are lined with metal so they reflect the waves around the oven.

Most microwaves have a rotating plate that turns the food so it cooks more evenly.

Microwaves don't get hot enough to brown food, so they aren't very good for cooking meat.

How they work

Something called a magnetron creates a fast-flipping magnetic field that forces water molecules in food to spin. These rotating molecules bump into each other, creating friction that **raises the temperature of food**. The effect barely penetrates the surface of the food, but the heat spreads to cook the rest.

Solar ovens

Microwave ovens use very little energy to cook food, but solar ovens use nothing but the sun! They can be as simple as a foil-lined box that reflects sunshine onto a pot. This heats up to cook food or heat water **without using any fuel or creating any polluting fumes**. Set up a solar oven outside and try melting marshmallows or cheese. Depending on the time of day and strength of the sun, it might take a while, but who cares? It's free!

0:00

The first microwave oven was around 6½ft (2m) tall!

Opening the door cuts off power to the magnetron and cuts off the magnetic field, stopping the cooking process.

Inventing the microwave

Microwave ovens were invented after World War II by Percy Spencer. He adapted wartime radar technology when he noticed microwaves from a radar he was working on **melted a chocolate bar in his pocket**. Within two years, his company, Raytheon, sold the first commercial microwave oven, costing the equivalent of $51,000 and weighing almost half a ton!

COOKING WITHOUT HEAT

Rollmop herrings
These pickled herrings have been popular in Europe since Medieval times. They are made by rolling herring fillets around a stuffing of onions, gherkins, or olives, then soaking them in water, vinegar, and salt.

There are lots of ways to "cook" or preserve food **without using heat**. Some of the tastiest foods are actually cooked with salt or smoke rather than heat, and the use of acids and sugars to pickle and preserve food has a long history. The processes mostly have the same aim: kill bacteria, break down proteins, change texture, and develop flavors.

Vegetables such as cucumbers, onions, peppers, and cabbage, as well as meats, fish, and eggs can all be pickled.

Ceviche

Ceviche

Pronounced "sevichay," this is a popular South American technique for cooking seafood using **citrus fruit**. The citric acid in lemons, limes, and oranges, effectively cooks the surface of the raw fish, kills bacteria, and adds zesty flavors.

Pickling

Pickling uses vinegar or salty water and other flavorings to break down food and **preserve it**. Pickling was initially used so there was always something to eat during the lean winter months, but now it's mainly used because people like the flavor.

Smoking

Smoking used to be an important step in the process of salting and drying fish. The fish was hung above a smoldering fire while smoke left deposits on the fish that helped **keep air and bacteria out**. In truth, smoke has limited preservation properties and is mainly there to add flavor.

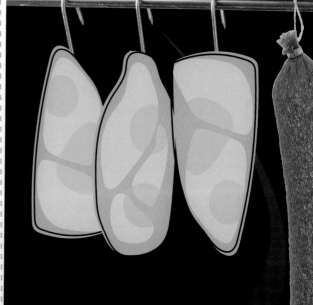

Modern smoked salmon is essentially raw fish that's been lightly smoked and salted, which is why it doesn't last very long in the fridge.

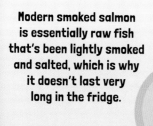

Air drying

Italian and Spanish hams and sausages are packed in salt for a few months to kill any bacteria, and then hung in a dark place with good ventilation for up to two years. The air **dehydrates** the meat, which takes on an intense flavor.

Salami slices

Gravlax
Gravlax is smoked salmon...without the smoke. Fillets of salmon are packed in a mix of salt, sugar, and herbs, for anywhere from twelve hours to several days. As the salt penetrates the fish, water is removed, intensifying the flavor. The salt prevents bacteria from multiplying, making the fish last longer.

Salami
Salami is made by finely chopping pork with pork fat, packing it into skins made from animal intestines, fermenting it, and drying it. Unusually for this type of non-cooking, bacteria are actively encouraged—as long as they are the right ones!

UNUSUAL FOODS

There are thousands of different foods in the world, and every country has rich cultural histories based around certain dishes or ingredients. Here are a few foods you **might not have heard of**. Not everybody will like them, but don't forget that different people have a different sense of taste.

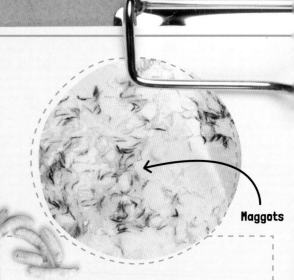

Maggots

Casu marzu

This cheese from Sardinia in Italy is super pungent, super tasty, and super hard to find. And for good reason—it contains **live maggots** that help give it flavour. It's banned by the European Food Safety Authority.

Gold leaf used as decoration.

Edible metal

Some metals are used as food additives, and have even been given E numbers to regulate their use. Gold is E175 and silver is E174. They are used to decorate food in an **extravagant gesture of wealth**. The metals are totally indigestible so they emerge intact from your behind. Gold leaf is very thin, and the amounts used are tiny, so you're unlikely to lay a golden egg. Sorry.

Fartichokes

Jerusalem artichokes are the **fartiest food on Earth**. They're packed with a sugar called inulin that doesn't break down in the small intestine. Instead, inulin makes its way to the large intestine, where bacteria feed on it and produce huge amounts of gas. Weirdly, Jerusalem artichokes aren't from Jerusalem, and aren't even artichokes (they're related to sunflowers).

Surströmming

These herrings have one of the most **revolting smells** of any food in the world, with the flavor of vomit, acid, and rotten fish. This Swedish delicacy is made by fermenting herrings for months. Cans often buckle due to the fermenting gases.

Margarine

Margarine was Invented in 1869 as a cheap **replacement for butter**. The original recipe used beef fat, milk, water, and cow udders. It's now made by adding lye, fuller's earth, hydrogen, and nickel to vegetable fat. Yum?

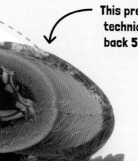

This preservation technique dates back 500 years.

Century eggs

This Chinese delicacy is made by **preserving eggs** in ash, salt, clay, calcium oxide, and rice hulls for several months (not 100 years!). This causes a series of chemical reactions, changing the egg white into a dark brown jelly and the yolk into a green cream. The eggs smell strongly rotten. They can be bought in Asian food stores across the world.

Square watermelons

In Japan, some watermelons are grown in square glass boxes. As they grow, the melons take the shape of the box. They don't taste any different, but it makes them **easier to stack and transport**.

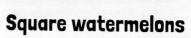

Which of these foods would you like to try the most? (Or least!)

VITAMINS AND MINERALS

You might have heard people say healthy foods contain vitamins and minerals—but we never get to see them. So what are they, and why are they invisible? Well, they're **micronutrients**, which means that although it's vital we eat them, we only need tiny amounts. There are a lot of different types, and luckily, they can be found in plenty of foods.

By eating a balanced diet you should get all the vitamins and minerals your body needs.

Vitamins

The word "vitamin" was coined by the brilliantly named Polish biochemist Casimir Funk. It refers to the thirteen essential micronutrients that humans need to survive, but **can't be created by our bodily processes**. This means that we need to consume them in food or drinks. Without them our bodies won't function properly.

Minerals are found in rocks and soil. Plants that grow in soil absorb the minerals through their roots. Then we eat the plants and absorb them.

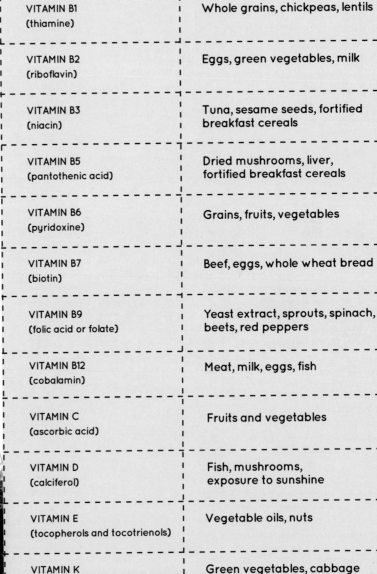

VITAMIN:	SOURCES:
VITAMIN A (retinols and carotenoids)	Carrots, liver, butter, eggs
VITAMIN B1 (thiamine)	Whole grains, chickpeas, lentils
VITAMIN B2 (riboflavin)	Eggs, green vegetables, milk
VITAMIN B3 (niacin)	Tuna, sesame seeds, fortified breakfast cereals
VITAMIN B5 (pantothenic acid)	Dried mushrooms, liver, fortified breakfast cereals
VITAMIN B6 (pyridoxine)	Grains, fruits, vegetables
VITAMIN B7 (biotin)	Beef, eggs, whole wheat bread
VITAMIN B9 (folic acid or folate)	Yeast extract, sprouts, spinach, beets, red peppers
VITAMIN B12 (cobalamin)	Meat, milk, eggs, fish
VITAMIN C (ascorbic acid)	Fruits and vegetables
VITAMIN D (calciferol)	Fish, mushrooms, exposure to sunshine
VITAMIN E (tocopherols and tocotrienols)	Vegetable oils, nuts
VITAMIN K (quinone)	Green vegetables, cabbage

Minerals

Minerals are **inorganic**, which means they can't be made of—or by—living matter. Most come from eating animals and plants, and from drinking water. Minerals perform a dizzying variety of functions in the body such as building and replacing bones and teeth, maintaining body fluid and tissue health, powering enzymes, and maintaining nerve functions.

There's enough iron in your body to make a nail around 3in (8cm) long!

MINERAL:	FUNCTION:	SOURCES:
CALCIUM	Bone and teeth health, muscle contraction	Milk, cheese, bread, leafy green veggies
PHOSPHORUS	Bone and cell health	Red meat, dairy, chicken, oats, rice
MAGNESIUM	Bone and tissues health, enzymes, muscles, and nerve health	Leafy green veggies, fish, nuts, bread, milk, cheese
SODIUM	Body water levels, electrolyte balance	Salty foods
POTASSIUM	Cell and nerve function, electrolyte and water balance	Meat, eggs, nuts, beans
SULFUR	Muscle health, cell repair, and enzyme health	Milk, cheese, bread, leafy green veggies
IRON	Transporting oxygen around the body, blood production, and helping the immune system	Cereals, vegetables, red meat, liver, eggs, pulses
FLUORIDE	Bone and teeth health	Toothpaste, fluorinated tap water
CHLORINE	Production of stomach acids, cell functions	Table salt
COPPER	Enzyme function	Liver, fish, nuts, seeds
ZINC	Enzyme function	Red meat, chicken, nuts, dairy
MANGANESE	Enzyme function	Grains, seeds, peas, leafy green veggies
MOLYBDENUM	Breaking down proteins	Peas, nuts, whole grains
IODINE	Hormone production	Seaweed, eggs, grains
CHROMIUM	Breaking down sugars and fats	Broccoli, red grape juice, meat
SELENIUM	Enzyme function	Brazil nuts, fish, meats, grains

FIND IRON IN YOUR CEREAL!

People say it's important to eat mineral-rich foods containing calcium, potassium, and zinc, but aren't those all metals? Well, many cereals do contain these metals but the quantities are too small to see or taste and we have to trust that they're in there. But scientists don't like to leave things to trust—**they want evidence!** Luckily, there's a metal you can prove is in your food: iron.

You will need

- 3½oz (100g) iron-rich cereal (check the list of ingredients!)
- Food processor
- Large, sealable plastic bag
- 1 pint (600ml) hot water
- Strong magnet
- Cutting board

! You'll need a powerful magnet for this, but you only need a small one. Strong magnets aren't toys, so you need to be careful with them.

1 Pour the cereal into a food processor and pulse until it turns to crumbs.

2 Put the crumbs in a strong, sealable plastic bag and add hot—not boiling—water. Mix together then seal the bag.

4 Lift the bag until you can see the magnet underneath, then lift both up together, keeping the magnet touching the bag. Slowly move the magnet across the bag to attract any floating iron particles. They're tiny, but you should soon be able to see a smudge of iron filings following the magnet!

3 Place the magnet on a cutting board and put the bag on top. Massage the bag gently to get the mush to move around, then leave for an hour.

Between 1978 and 1980, French entertainer Michel Lotito, also known as Monsieur Mangetout ("Mr. Eats-All") managed to eat a whole **Cessna 150 airplane**! He cut it into pieces and was able to eat it because he had a very strong stomach lining. DON'T try to copy him. You'll hurt yourself very badly.

WHY DOES POPCORN POP?

That popping sound you hear when you cook popcorn is part of what makes it so much fun! But have you ever thought about what causes that noise? There is a lot of science at work behind that pop **pop POPPING**.

POP!

POP!

Steam expanding in the kernel

Kernel

What's popping?

Inside each popcorn kernel is a starchy filling and a droplet of water. When the kernels are heated, the water turns to steam and **builds pressure** in the shell. When the shell can no longer take the pressure, the starchy center explodes with a POP, resulting in the tasty popcorn we love to eat.

There are four main types of corn: dent corn, flint corn, sweet corn, and popcorn.

Popping corn

Popcorn kernels have a hard shell but are soft inside. They are the only type of corn that pops. If you cook sweet corn this way it will just turn soft and mushy.

POP!

When the kernels get hot enough, they explode.

Make your own popcorn

You will need:

- 1 tbsp oil • 2oz (60g) popcorn
- 2oz (60g) butter • wooden spoon
- saucepan with lid

1

Heat oil in a pan over medium heat and add the corn. Stir to coat in the oil and place the lid on top. Listen. Can you hear the pops?

2

After a few minutes the popping will stop. Turn off the heat then stir in the butter. It's ready to eat!

Taking it further

If you experiment with these variables you might get different results:

- Cook the corn at a lower temperature. Were more kernels left unpopped?

- Add flavors such as sugar, salt, caramel, or spices. Which batch tasted best?

What is gum made of?

The chewy part of gum is called gum base. It's a mix of **polymers** (long-chain molecules that stick together in interesting ways) including resin (for the chewy feel), and wax softeners and elastomers (for flexibility). Other ingredients add sweetness, flavor, color, and glycerine, which keeps the gum soft.

A study of London's Oxford Street in England found 250,000 pieces of gum stuck to the ground!

THE STICKY SCIENCE OF GUM

Gum is amazing stuff that's designed to be **chewed for ages without changing**. Humans have been chewing gum-like substances for thousands of years to keep our teeth clean, breath fresh, or simply for the sense of pleasure we get from chewing.

Bubble gum contains more elastic polymers than chewing gum. This means it can stretch farther before collapsing.

POP!

Is it safe to eat?

Gum isn't designed to be swallowed, and has no nutritional value, but the stories about it **staying in your stomach for years** aren't true—it's a type of fiber and passes through you just like the rest of your food. It's still not a good idea to swallow lots, though—it can stick to other foods and form a blockage in your intestines.

The first chewing gum marketed in the USA was produced in 1848 from tree sap, but by the 1960s gum makers had created a synthetic rubber which was much cheaper.

Historical gum

The earliest known "gum" is a 6,000-year-old lump of birch bark tar with teeth marks in it found in Finland. A lot of ancient peoples made gum, including the Ancient Greeks who used gum made from the resin of the **mastic tree**.

Mastic leaves

Make a piece of gum disappear!

Gum is powerful stuff, but you can make it dissolve in your mouth by **chewing it with chocolate**. Gum is hydrophobic (it repels water), which is why it stays chewy in your saliva, but chocolate contains cocoa butter fats that dissolve the gum. Chew them together and bingo: that rubbery gum turns to liquid and vanishes!

 + = Poof!

WATER IS WONDERFUL

Water is tasteless, colorless, and odorless. But it's also incredibly important. In fact, it's so important that every single form of life on Earth **needs it to survive**.

H
Hydrogen atom

If this big circle was an oxygen atom...

What is water?

If you could zoom in so close to a drop of water that you could see the atoms inside it (which you can't because they're MUCH too small), you'd find that it's made up of trillions of tiny molecules. Each of these molecules is made up of **two small hydrogen** atoms and **one larger oxygen atom**. This is why the chemical symbol for water is H_2O.

O
Oxygen atom

H
Hydrogen atom

and the two little circles were hydrogen atoms...you'd have water!

Why we need water

Around **60 percent of the human body is water**, and every cell in every organ needs it to work properly. It's vital that we keep matching our water intake to the amount that we lose from sweat and urine throughout the day.

How much do we need?

Everyone's water requirements are different, but most 9–13 year-olds need around 3½ pints (2 liters) a day, although a lot of that comes from food (fruit and vegetables are about 75 percent water). But drinking water is very good for you, so it's okay to drink more—especially if it's hot or you've been active.

Make a bottle vortex

Anything that spins around an axis is called a vortex, and you can create one very easily using water. Fill a bottle with water and seal the lid. Turn it upside down over a sink and swirl the bottle around until the water inside is spinning. Now carefully unscrew the lid and watch the whirlpool you've created as it drains out.

The spinning water creates a cool effect.

We can survive without food for around three weeks, but without water we would die from dehydration in just a few days.

What's happening?

Swirling the bottle sets the water in motion but when it drains out, something cool happens. As the water at the widest part of the bottle gets closer to the opening, it spins even faster. This is because of something called the **conservation of angular momentum**. All that really means here is the closer to the middle of the bottle the water gets, the faster it has to spin. The same thing happens when water goes down the drain, and it's the same science behind things like tornadoes and spiral galaxies!

41

FIZZY COLA

Cola has an unusual flavor—it's hard to describe and there's nothing else quite like it. But if you **make your own version**, you begin to understand exactly why it tastes like it does. Your version won't look or taste quite the same as the big brands, but it's surprisingly close.

Where do the bubbles come from?

Cola manufacturers use machines to **force CO_2 gas** into sweet liquid at very high pressure and very low temperature. The pressure and cold maximize the amount of CO_2 that can be dissolved in the liquid. You can buy home versions of these to make any drink fizzy.

Why do we love fizzy drinks?

Fizzy drinks excite our senses. When you open a fizzy drink, your sense of hearing sends messages to your brain, which reacts with pleasure to the hiss of gas. That hiss is the sound of carbon dioxide (CO_2) pushing through the opening and sending flavorful smells into the air. When we sip, our taste receptors are excited by the sourness created by the CO_2, the sweetness of the drink, and the pleasurable touch sensations from the bubbles and coldness of the liquid.

Try a taste test between flat and fizzy cola. You'll find the difference created by the bubbles is very dramatic.

You will need

- 16 fl oz (500 ml) water
- 1 lb 10 oz (750 g) sugar
- Zest and juice of 2 limes
- Zest and juice of 2 oranges
- Zest and juice of 2 lemons
- ½ tsp vanilla extract
- ½ tsp nutmeg powder
- ½ tsp cinnamon powder
- ½ tsp coriander powder
- Large pan
- Spoon
- Clean tea towel or cheesecloth
- Sieve
- Bowl
- Bottle or jar
- Fizzy water

Most fizzy drinks are packed with sugar, which is bad for your teeth because it feeds the bacteria that cause tooth decay.

Put all the ingredients except the fizzy water into a pan. Heat and stir until the sugar has dissolved. Turn the heat off and allow to cool.

Fizzy explosions

If you have a big backyard and are **allowed to make a mess**, try this: Drop a few Mentos mints into a large bottle of diet cola, stand back, and watch the fizzy explosion. Mentos have a surface that **encourages bubbles** to form, and the reaction feeds on itself—one bubble helps to create more bubbles. Also, as the Mentos drop straight to the bottom of the bottle, it maximizes the distance the bubbles rise, forming more bubbles as they go until they erupt!

Any fizzy drink will work, but diet drinks that use sugar substitutes seem to work best.

Beverage companies add extra ingredients for color and flavor. The recipe for Coca Cola is so secret that according to the company, only two employees know the entire thing.

2

Lay a tea towel over a sieve and place over a bowl. Pour the liquid through it to strain out all the pieces. Discard them and keep the syrup.

3

To make a glass of cola, fill a glass with one part syrup to six parts fizzy water (or adapt to your taste). It tastes best served with ice.

INSTANT ICE CREAM

Need ice cream fast? Feeling lazy? Got some frozen strawberries? This super-fast recipe is so simple it's almost embarrassing. All you need to do is keep some strawberries in the freezer in case of an ice cream emergency and **let science do the hard work** for you!

You will need

- 1lb 2oz (500g) strawberries
- 9fl oz (250ml) cold plain yogurt or heavy cream
- 2 tbsp honey
- Food processor

If you're not a fan of strawberries, almost any frozen fruit should work. Experiment to see which is your favorite.

1

Carefully remove the stalks from the strawberries and give them a quick chop. Put them in the freezer until totally frozen. (Or just cheat and buy frozen ones!)

2

Put the frozen strawberries in a food processor with the yogurt and honey. Carefully blend everything together until smooth then add your favorite toppings and serve. Thanks, science!

During World War II some American fighter pilots made DIY ice cream by strapping cans filled with ice cream mixture to their planes. They had an internal stirrer attached to a small propeller that turned in the air and agitated the liquid as it froze at high altitude.

The science

Ice cream is a **colloidal emulsion**—it contains milk fats mixed with milk protein, sugar, air, and ice (frozen water). After the ingredients are mixed it must be frozen quickly because slow freezing creates large, crunchy ice crystals that aren't very pleasant to eat. Fast freezing, on the other hand, creates a lot of much smaller crystals, creating that smooth texture we know and love.

Ice crystals

Sugar

Fat

Air

Why it works

The cold from the strawberries is just enough to freeze the other ingredients, and the power of the food processor can force fat and water (which normally don't mix well) to blend, mixing the fat in the yogurt or cream with the iced water inside the strawberries.

The Ancient Greeks are thought to have eaten an ice cream like mixture of snow, honey, and fruit. But ice cream was probably invented around 500BCE in Asia.

45

DRINKS THAT GLOW!

Some foods and drinks fluoresce, which means they glow. Obviously, lots of things look brighter if you point a light at them, but fluorescence is particularly cool because you can point an invisible beam of **UV light** at something that then visibly glows. Fill a glass with tonic water, turn out the lights, and point a UV flashlight at it. Thanks to an ingredient called quinine, it will glow!

You will need

- Glass
- Tonic water
- Ultraviolet (UV) flashlight
- Salt (optional)

What's happening?

It's all about **quantum mechanics**, the physics that describes the very smallest energy levels in atomic and subatomic particles. Even powerful microscopes can't see these tiny particles—so we have to **imagine** what's going on.

UV flashlights are often sold to storekeepers to check if paper money is real. Turn out the lights and use your flashlight to see if any of the food in your kitchen glows.

Salt

When the quinine molecules in the tonic water are hit with UV light, they absorb the beam's energy and become unstable. To stop this, they immediately "relax," and release the extra energy as another beam of light. However, during the process, a little of the **invisible UV light** has been transformed, and is released as **visible light** instead.

If you sprinkle salt into the tonic water, it disrupts the glow and turns it off.

EXPLODING FOOD!

Have you ever eaten **popping candy** and wondered what causes the sensation as it dissolves in your mouth? Although it may seem like thousands of little chemical reactions going off on your tongue, it's actually a lot of tiny explosions.

Little explosions

The explosions on your tongue are simply little pockets of **carbon dioxide gas** (CO_2) breaking out of sugar. The gas bubbles are trapped in the candy under pressure and as the saliva in your mouth dissolves the sugar, the brittle casings burst, at which point the gas expands with a little "pop".

Close-up of popping candy

It sounds odd to add gas to food but it's pretty common. If you see "E290" on an ingredients label, that's CO_2!

Carbon dioxide (CO_2)

Water

Sugar

CO_2

How is it made?

Popping candy is made by first mixing water with sugar and heating it so most of the water dissolves, creating "hard crack sugar." Carbon dioxide gas (CO_2) is then mixed into it, and left to cool under pressure. As it cools, the sugar molecules set and the carbon dioxide bubbles get **trapped inside**. It's then ground into crumbs and put in a packet.

Sweet and safe

You may have heard rumors that eating popping candy with a fizzy drink will make your **stomach explode!** It's not true, but when popping candy was first sold the myth was so widespread the creators had to release advertisements denying it.

Popping candy was created in 1961 by Leon Kremzner and William Mitchell, two chemists working for the General Foods company.

COOL CABBAGE

Vegetables have a reputation for being boring, but that couldn't be more wrong! There are amazing stories to be found lurking behind any food if you look hard enough. Take a close look at a savoy cabbage. If it has a light dusty-looking coating, you're looking at a very sophisticated **superhydrophobic nano-coating** that stops the cabbage from getting too wet—and rotting—while it's growing.

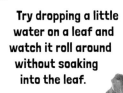

Try dropping a little water on a leaf and watch it roll around without soaking into the leaf.

Lotus leaf   Water droplets

Super...what?

If you break down the word "superhydrophobic," it technically means **"very scared of water,"** but in reality, it means "very difficult to soak." The effect is seen on cabbages and on the leaves of the lotus plant, which grows in water and needs protection to avoid rotting.

What's going on?

A cabbage's superhydrophobic coating is made up of a network of hundreds of thousands of tiny wax bumps that develop on the surface of the leaves. When water hits this coating it is repelled by the wax structure, beads up into a droplet, and rolls off.

Cabbage close-up

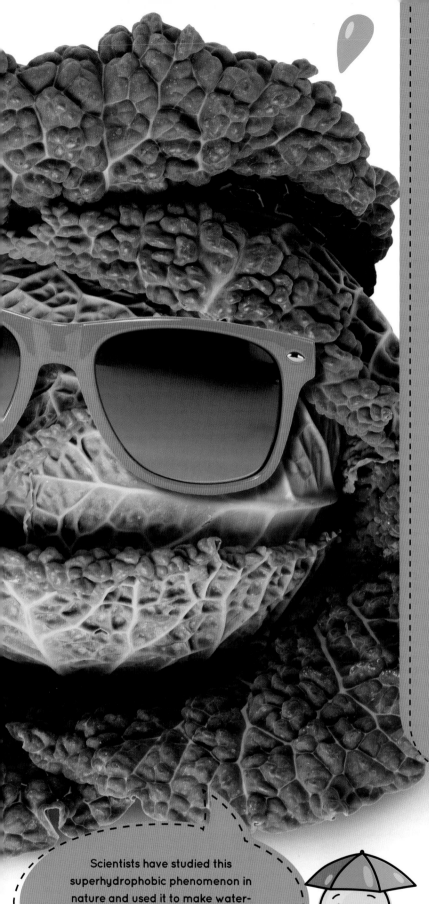

See for yourself

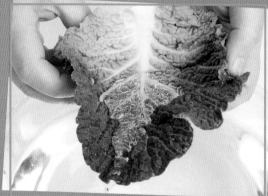

Take a savoy cabbage leaf and dip it in a bowl of water. You should see the water pooling around the structure. Lift it out. The cabbage will be dry.

Now wipe and scratch the leaf with your thumb and dip it in again. This time the cabbage leaf will get wet. You have broken the coating, making it no longer superhydrophobic.

What's a nano-structure?

A nano-structure is a **very, very small** structure. You can see the effect of superhydrophobic nano-structures by looking at water on a cabbage leaf, but to see the nano-structures themselves you need an extremely powerful microscope called a scanning electron microscope (SEN).

Scientists have studied this superhydrophobic phenomenon in nature and used it to make water-repellent and self-cleaning technology for everything from clothing to windows.

51

The pH Scale

Acids and their chemical opposites, **bases** (sometimes called alkalines), are measured using the pH scale with water (neutral) in the middle at pH 7, acids at one end down to pH 1, and alkalines at the other end up to pH 14.

Orange juice

Chocolate

Butter

ACIDS (1–6)

| 0 Strong acid | 1 | 2 | 3 | 4 | 5 | 6 |

SOUR SCIENCE

A lot of food, especially fruit, is naturally acidic. When this acid touches your tongue, your taste receptors send signals to your brain that make you experience **sourness**. Fruit such as lemons, limes, and grapefruits are packed with citric acid, which is what makes them taste sour. The acid works as a preservative in the fruit, slowing down the growth of bacteria so it doesn't rot too quickly.

Strong acids are corrosive, which means they can destroy substances, including metal. NEVER touch or taste non-food acids.

Is it safe?

A lot of foods contain acids, and are perfectly safe to eat because they are relatively weak. Many of us enjoy the taste of sourness from acids, and it's common to add vinegar to sauces or squeeze lemon juice over a dish before eating it.

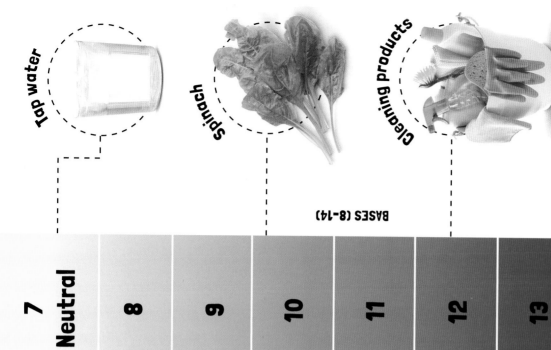

Tap water

Spinach

Cleaning products

Alkaline food

There aren't many alkaline foods, but baking soda, which is added to bread and cakes to help them rise, is very alkaline.

BASES (8–14)

| 7 Neutral | 8 | 9 | 10 | 11 | 12 | 13 | Strong base 14 |

Fizzy sherbet: edible chemistry!

What happens when acids and bases meet? Well, when citric acid is added to baking soda, and water is added to allow them to mix, a fizzing **"acid-base reaction"** occurs. The acid and baking soda neutralize each other and create a salt called sodium citrate as a by-product. It may sound scary, but it's not—it's just what happens when sherbet fizzes on our tongue! If you look at the ingredient list of sherbet you should see both citric acid (an acid), and bicarbonate of soda (a base), alongside various other flavorings and sweeteners.

Eating sherbet creates this amazing chemical reaction:

$$C_6H_8O_7 + 3NaHCO_3 \longrightarrow 3CO_2 + 3H_2O + C_6H_5O_7Na_3$$

Vitamin C

Many fruit and vegetables contain ascorbic acid (also known as vitamin C). It's essential for a healthy diet and helps maintain our immune system. If you don't eat enough vitamin C you can get a very unpleasant disease called **scurvy**, which is something pirates and sailors used to suffer from due to poor diet while at sea.

Sailors and pirates were given limes to prevent scurvy, but black currants would have been better because they contain a lot more vitamin C.

53

COLOR-CHANGING CABBAGE

Think cabbage isn't special? Think again! Cabbages contain clever ingredients called anthocyanins that change color when mixed with an **acid or an alkaline solution**. Amaze your friends by making color-changing liquids from an "ordinary" cabbage!

You will need

- 3½oz (100g) red cabbage, cut into pieces
- Food processor
- 3½fl oz (100ml) water
- Bowl
- Sieve
- Spoon
- Large jar or glass, filled ¾ of the way with water
- 1 lemon, cut into quarters
- 1 tsp powdered laundry detergent

1

Put the cabbage in a food processor with 3½fl oz (100ml) water. Carefully blend it up.

2

Strain the mixture through a sieve into a bowl. Keep the colored juice and discard the mush.

3

Add a splash of the juice to the jar of water and stir. You need just enough to create a ghostly purple color. Now taste it.

The anthocyanins in red cabbage are a **pH indicator**, which means they change color when mixed with either an acidic or alkaline substance. Lemon makes the mixture acidic, so the anthocyanins turn from purple to pink, and the laundry detergent is alkaline, which first neutralizes the acid, then turns the liquid alkaline, changing its color as it does.

4

Squeeze a lemon quarter into the purple juice and stir it. It should turn pink. Now taste it again.

5

Add 1 tsp of laundry detergent to the jar and watch as it falls to the bottom of the glass. It will begin to turn the juice blue and then to a light greenish color. **DON'T TASTE THIS ONE.**

!

Warning
Do NOT drink this solution—detergent powder is VERY toxic.

INVISIBLE INK

The practice of hiding messages or images so nobody knows they are there is called steganography. There are a lot of very complicated ways to do this, but you can use the power of food and science to create your own with ease.

Other invisible inks

Lemon juice isn't the only way to make invisible ink with food. You can also use diluted honey, but for different reasons. When the honey caramelizes it turns brown and shows up. You can also write a message using tonic water that will glow under UV light.

1 Squeeze the lemon juice into a bowl then use it to write or draw a secret message onto paper. Leave it to dry and turn invisible.

2 Place your message over a towel or ironing board and carefully apply heat from an iron until your message appears.

What's happening?

When you heat the paper, the organic substances in the lemon juice will **break down** and turn brown while the rest of the paper stays white, revealing the message. If you have a UV flashlight, you can use it to reveal a tonic water message, then turn the flashlight off to make it invisible again.

Hidden messages have been around for centuries. Guy Fawkes' Gunpowder Plot in 1605 in England was exposed by the interception of messages written in orange juice, and lemon juice was used by spies in World War I.

Why not write a hidden message for your friends and tell them how to reveal it?

INSIDE AN EGG

Eggs squeeze a huge amount of science into a **simple-looking package**. Fertilized eggs contain everything required to create an animal, but the eggs we eat are unfertilized. Eggs are full of protein, are essential for batters and many baked foods, can be used to lighten food, and help to create emulsions like mayonnaise. Oh, and they're great scrambled, fried, poached, or boiled!

There are 20 billion chickens in the world (almost three for every human) and each one produces around 300 eggs a year. That's more than 1 TRILLION total.

Surprisingly strong shell

Eggs are protected by brittle shells that crack easily if their **sides** are knocked. But, try holding an egg at the **top and bottom** between your forefinger and thumb. Now squeeze. You'll find they are extremely difficult, if not impossible, to break. Their dome shape spreads the pressure across a wide surface area and gives it a lot of strength. This is why many buildings have dome-shaped roofs.

Test how fresh an egg is by putting it in water. Older eggs will float and fresh eggs will sink. Eggs lose moisture and absorb air as they get older. Eventually they become less dense than water, and will float.

Shell

The hard outer shell of an egg is made of calcium carbonate crystals. It's porous, with up to 17,000 tiny holes that allow air and moisture to pass through it.

Membranes

Just under the eggshell are the inner and outer membranes, which are also porous but protect the egg against bacteria. These membranes are easily spotted under the shell of a boiled egg, and look a little like plastic wrap. They are partly made of keratin, the same substance in human hair.

Outer membrane

Shell

Inner membrane

Chalazae

These little "ropes" of tougher egg white keep the yolk in the center of the egg.

Yolk

Yolks contain less water, more protein, and lot more fat than the egg whites. The proteins coagulate (thicken and turn solid) at 158°F (70°C).

Vitelline membrane
This thin casing contains the yolk.

Albumen

The white, or albumen, is mostly water, but also contains proteins. The proteins coagulate and turn white at 149°F (65°C).

Air cell

The inside of an egg cools and contracts after the egg is laid, so an air cell forms to equalize the pressure. It sits between the membranes. As the egg gets older it loses moisture and the air cell grows to make up for this.

Ostriches lay the largest eggs of any bird, around 6in (15cm) long.

You will need

- An egg
- Glass or jar
- Vinegar (any type will do)
- Plastic wrap
- Bowl
- Flashlight (optional)

NAKED EGGS

Yes, you really can strip the shell off an egg but keep the insides intact—leaving you with a large, bouncy, squishy egg. It takes around three days to do so, but it's a very cool example of an **acid-base reaction**. Don't eat the egg afterward, it's still raw—and very disgusting!

It's a good idea to make more than one naked eggs at a time in case one breaks while you're cleaning it.

1

DAY 1:
Place the egg in the glass and pour vinegar on top until submerged. Look at the egg, it will become covered in bubbles. Cover with plastic wrap and poke a hole in the top.

2

DAY 2:
The next day, the egg will look bigger and the outer shell will have started to disintegrate. Pour the old vinegar out and replace with fresh vinegar. Cover with plastic wrap again and store.

If you hold a flashlight up to the egg you'll be able to clearly see the yolk.

What's happening?

Eggshells are made of calcium carbonate, which is slightly alkaline. This reacts with the acetic acid in the vinegar, creating bubbles and breaking down the shell. What's left behind is the egg's **membrane**, which is soft, but strong enough to hold the liquid egg inside.

DAY 3:
By now the hard outer shell should be gone. If the egg is soft, wash it carefully under cold water, gently rubbing off the last harder pieces. If it's not, replace the vinegar and leave for another day.

Once the hard shell is gone, you can squish and even bounce your egg. But do this over a bowl or tray—it's still liquid inside!

Membrane

Raw egg

BRILLIANT BREAD

Bread has been one of humanity's most important foods for **thousands of years**, providing more nutrients to the world population than any other food. Why? Well, it's mostly made from wheat, which is an easily grown, easily stored, and easily cooked ingredient that contains a huge amount of energy.

CO_2

The importance of bread

Bread became the building block of human nutrition thousands of years ago, when life was lived in a near-constant state of hunger. Whenever people suffered drought, war, or natural disaster, a shortage of wheat could cause famine. It's so important that shortages of bread have caused riots, strikes, and revolutions that have greatly changed the course of history.

What are all those holes?

Take a close look at a slice of crusty bread and you should be able to see thousands of tiny holes. These holes are what gives bread it's **light, fluffy interior**. They are usually made by yeast—millions of microscopic cells that create a lot of tiny bubbles of carbon dioxide gas (CO_2).

Loaves of bread are leavened (lightened and softened by adding yeast or another ingredient), but many people eat unleavened flatbreads.

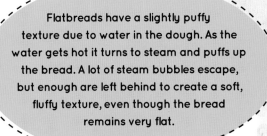

Flatbreads have a slightly puffy texture due to water in the dough. As the water gets hot it turns to steam and puffs up the bread. A lot of steam bubbles escape, but enough are left behind to create a soft, fluffy texture, even though the bread remains very flat.

Types of bread

There are hundreds of types of bread, ranging from long, crusty French wheat flour baguettes, to fluffy, holey, pancake-like Ethiopian teff-flour injera. The most basic bread recipes can contain just **flour and water**, but other ingredients are often added for flavor or texture. The dough is then cooked using intense heat to first soften the flour and then harden it to give a good structure.

The word "companion" means "person to share bread with."

Any type of flour can be used to make bread. Flour is just a word for a powder made by grinding down hard, dry grains or roots. Potato, corn, and rice flour all make great bread.

Holes created by carbon dioxide

Gluten

Bakers are obsessed with gluten, a type of protein found in flours that gives dough **elasticity**. This helps the bread to rise and form by trapping the carbon dioxide bubbles created by cooking so they don't escape before the bread hardens. Gluten also helps to give the cooked bread a great chewy texture.

WHAT MAKES BREAD RISE?

Have you ever eaten a flaky croissant, a slice of bread, or a fluffy English muffin and wondered what you need to thank for turning the thick, heavy dough into something so light, fluffy, and delicious? Well it's all because of teeny-tiny creatures called **yeast**. By using balloons we can watch the yeast at work.

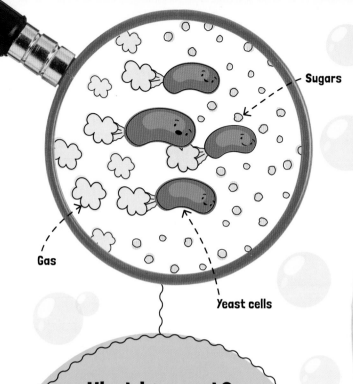

Sugars

Gas

Yeast cells

What is yeast?

Yeast cells are tiny, single-celled organisms that feed on the sugars in flour and produce huge amounts of tiny **carbon dioxide and ethanol gas bubbles** as a by-product. The yeast is killed during cooking, but the bubbles get trapped in the dough, leaving behind the holes that give bread its lovely texture. Without yeast, bread would be a big, heavy, uneven lump.

You will need

- 4 tsp instant yeast
- 2 small bottles
- 3 tsp sugar
- 2 balloons
- Lukewarm water
- Measuring cup

Yeast-inflated balloons

Put 2 tsp of yeast into each bottle and label them A and B. Put 3 tsp of sugar into bottle B, and pour 3½ fl oz (100 ml) of warm water into each bottle. Give the bottles a good swirl, then put a balloon over each one. Now wait for about an hour to see what happens.

A

What's happening?

Yeast needs energy, and sugar contains a lot of it. But when the yeast breaks sugar down, it produces waste products, one of which is the gas carbon dioxide (CO_2). As the yeast feasts on the sugar in bottle B, it **creates enough carbon dioxide** to inflate the balloon, but as bottle A has no sugar, the yeast can't produce gas and the balloon doesn't inflate.

B

Yeast cells are so small you can't see them, but just one teaspoonful of yeast powder has millions of the cells.

Proofing

It takes time for yeast to produce enough gas to make dough rise. When yeast is added to dough, it's often **left for an hour** or more to let the yeast get to work. This step is called proofing. Take a look at the same dough before, during, and after the yeast are done eating and producing their gases.

Before

During

After

RIPENING BANANAS

Bananas are amazing fruit. When a banana decides it's the right time to start ripening, it releases **ethylene gas**. This triggers a sequence of changes that develops flavors, softens the fruit, and starts the transformation of dull starchy carbohydrates into sweet-tasting sugars.

Bananas are very slightly radioactive, but don't worry, they're totally safe. Nuclear radiation levels are sometimes measured using "banana equivalent dose."

1 Unripe bananas are green from the chlorophyll that helps grow the plant. Green bananas taste dull and pasty because the carbohydrates have not yet broken down into sugars.

Many people disagree about which ripeness of banana is the best. Which is your favorite?

In a green banana, 36 percent of the carbohydrates are sugar...

2 Underripe bananas begin to turn yellow as chlorophyll breaks down, but they still don't have sweet, tasty flesh. It's at this stage that ethylene gas production surges.

...but that rises to 89 percent in a riper banana.

Most people peel bananas starting from the stalk, but monkeys are the real experts. If you watch monkeys, you'll see it's easier to pinch and peel them from the opposite end!

Plantain

148 million tons of bananas are grown every year, making them one of the world's most popular fruits. Strictly speaking, they are a type of berry, and they come in two main types: sweet bananas, and less sweet but still very tasty "plantains," which are used for cooking. The leaves of the banana plant are sometimes used as plates.

3 Ripe bananas develop brown speckles. Ripe bananas taste sweet due to high sugar levels, and have a soft, chewy texture and a very fruity smell.

4 Overripe bananas have black, marked skins and mushy flesh. They now release little or no ethylene, but will continue to ripen until they turn black and become rotten.

Overripe bananas are the best to bake with since they're packed with flavor.

Sharing the skill

Bananas produce such a high amount of ethylene gas, that underripe ones can be used to speed up the **ripening of other fruit** by being placed nearby. Overripe bananas produce very little ethylene, so are little use in helping to ripen other fruit.

GOOD AND BAD MOLD

Mold sounds bad, doesn't it? That fluffy growth is a pretty clear indication that your food has gone bad, but mold can also be a **very useful** tool. Mold is important for making food and drinks: Some cheese, soy sauce, cured meats such as pepperoni and salami, and wine rely on mold production for developing their flavors. And penicillin, one of the world's most important antibiotic medicines, is produced using the same strains of mold that are used to give blue cheeses their flavor.

What is mold?

Although they are often found together, mold is very different from bacteria. Mold blooms are made up of millions of microscopic fungi related to mushrooms. The white fuzzy part is made of tiny interconnected tubes, and the colored dusty part is made of the spores created by the mold in order to reproduce. **Molds feed on organic matter** and as they grow they produce enzymes that start breaking down that organic matter, making it rot and go bad.

Penicillin

Close-up of mold spores

Severely rotten bread that has been overtaken by mold.

Fresh bread.

Good mold

Some cheeses are **mixed with mold on purpose** to develop flavor. British Stilton, Danish Blue, and French Roquefort all have spores added at the start of the cheesemaking process. Once the cheese is a few weeks old and starts to form a crust, it is pierced with needles to create holes that allow the mold to grow and create the traditional blue veins. These holes give the mold access into the cheese, softening it, and developing flavors.

Some experts claim that strong blue cheeses can cause vivid dreams, but the science isn't very conclusive.

Roquefort

Bread being broken down by mold spores.

Storing food in cold, dark places slows down the growth of mold. That's why food lasts longer in the fridge.

Pepperoni

Bad mold

Take a deep breath. You've just breathed in nitrogen, oxygen, carbon dioxide, and almost certainly **mold spores**. In small quantities they cause no problems, but in certain conditions toxic molds can cause allergic reactions, breathing problems, coughs, headaches, and itchy eyes. They thrive in damp, dark, places around the house especially corners of bathrooms, kitchens, and cupboards. If the wrong ones infect stored food they can be very dangerous.

WHEN FOOD IS DANGEROUS

We need to eat to live, but the **same food that keeps us alive can sometimes be deadly**. Some plants, animals, and fungi contain toxic compounds that need to be removed, processed or cooked carefully, and badly stored food can contain dangerous levels of bacteria. Some foods may be perfectly fine for one person to eat but deadly for someone else. This is why it's vital that we all know the ingredients in the food we're eating.

Poisons

The science of poisons is called toxicology, and its main principle is that **there is a safe and unsafe level of every substance on Earth**. For example, water is essential to life and perfectly safe, but it is possible to drink too much. Apples contain potentially deadly cyanide but only in tiny amounts, and they contain a lot of vitamins and fiber, so they balance out as a healthy food. Food can also become poisonous through bad preparation or poor storage that allow microbes to thrive.

Allergies don't just come from food. Many people are allergic to stings, bites, medicines, pollen, and pet hair.

The most common food allergies and intolerances are:

Peanuts · Tree nuts such

Allergies

The complexity of the human body and vast range of chemical compounds in our food means you can have an allergic reaction to almost anything—or nothing. The reactions from food allergies range from mild skin irritation to severe anaphylaxis, which can be deadly. These reactions are caused by the body's immune system (our defense against infection) **mistakenly treating food as a threat**. It's not yet understood why people develop allergies.

Other dangerous foods

Fugu is a fish eaten as a delicacy in Japan. The flesh is safe to eat, but there's poison in the liver. If this contaminates the flesh it can catastrophically affect the nervous system, paralyzing muscles, and killing the victim. It's heavily regulated today, but it's estimated that 176 people died from fugu poisoning in 1958.

Fugu

The Korean delicacy san-nakji is made with very small octopuses. The suction cups on the octopus's arms still suck even after death, and can get stuck in the throat after swallowing. This problem causes around six deaths a year.

Intolerances

Food intolerances are a different problem than allergies. They're not life-threatening, and don't involve the immune system. They are usually caused by a **difficulty digesting certain foods**, which results in unpleasant physical reactions ranging from slight discomfort, to diarrhea, stomach cramps, and bloating. The most common causes are dairy products, wheat, and caffeine.

as walnuts and pecans · Fish · Shellfish · Eggs · Milk · Soy · Wheat · Mustard · Celery

HOT STUFF

If you've ever bitten into a spicy chili pepper, you'll know they can make your mouth feel like it's burning. But the pepper **isn't actually hot**, it's just a trick being played on your brain.

A general rule with chilis is the small ones are hotter than the big ones.

The science of spice

Peppers taste spicy because of a chemical inside them called **capsaicin.** Capsaicin reacts with the nerve endings in your mouth, throat, and skin, causing a reaction that feels like burning. Your brain reacts like a fire brigade to fight the hot sensation and flush it out by raising your heartbeat, making you sweat, and causing your eyes to water.

Signal to brain

Chili

Measuring heat

A pepper's spiciness is measured on the **Scoville scale.** The numbers on the scale relate to how many parts of water are needed to dilute a drop of the chili solution until the heat is undetectable. However, every chili is different, so the scale is only a rough guide.

Habanero

Bird's eye chili

Cayenne

Super hot

Around **100,000** Scoville units

Very hot

Around **50,000** Scoville units

Jalapeño

Poblano

Bell pepper

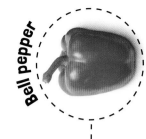

Hot
Around **5,000** Scoville units

Mild
Around **2,000** Scoville units

No heat
0 Scoville units

A fiery defense

The hottest parts of a chili are the **seeds** and **membrane**, because they contain the most capsaicin. This is part of a defensive trick the plant uses to stops animals destroying them, which would stop the chilis from being able to reproduce.

Tame the flame

You might be tempted to drink water when you suffer a chili's burning sensation, but this only spreads the reaction around your mouth and makes it worse because capsaicin doesn't dissolve in water. Fatty dairy products such as yogurt or milk do a better job of cooling down the heat because capsaicin DOES dissolve in fat.

In small doses, many people like the burning sensation from eating chilis.

Birds are immune to the effects of chilis. Scientists think it's because their taste buds can't detect capsaicin.

WHY DO ONIONS MAKE US CRY?

Onions are vital to many of the world's most popular dishes, but can deliver a nasty chemical poke in the eye to any chef that slices them. It's a clever **chemical defense mechanism** that stops animals from eating them in the fields. It's also lucky for us, because once cooked, these chemicals transform into a different set chemicals that give onions a delicious sweet flavor.

Humans enjoy the flavors in onions so much we grow nearly 100 million tons of them a year, making it a very successful plant. Clever onion.

More defenses

Onions aren't the only plant with a defensive skill. It's the reason that chilis taste spicy, and a lot of other vegetables have unique traits that can make them irritating (or poisonous) to predators, including humans.

Cassava

Cassava is highly poisonous due to cyanide compounds. The levels get particularly high in them during times of drought. But these compounds are destroyed by soaking and cooking, making cassava totally safe to eat.

Raw kidney beans

Raw kidney beans contain a highly toxic chemical called phytohaemagglutinin. Just four or five raw beans can cause sickness and diarrhea. It's deactivated when they are properly cooked, but great care should be taken with them.

Gas that makes you cry!

What's the cause?

When onions are sliced, the knife cuts through thousands of tiny cells, making a lot of different chemicals mix together. As they mix, an irritating chemical gas is created that floats into your eyes. Nerves sense the gas and send a message to your brain that an irritant is in the eye. The brain sends a message to your tear ducts signaling them to produce tears **to flush out the irritant**. Suddenly, you're crying.

Mushrooms

Poisonous mushrooms such as the Death Cap, Autumn Skullcap, Deadly Dapperling, and Destroying Angel are extremely toxic. They are really dangerous because they can look similar to edible ones. Never eat a mushroom you find in the wild.

Rhubarb

Rhubarb stalks make a wonderful crumble but the leaves contain a lot of oxalic acid, which can cause kidney problems and make you very sick. Luckily the leaves are extremely sour, so you're unlikely to eat them anyway.

Seeds and pits

The seeds and pits of fruit such as apples, apricots, peaches, and plums, contain poisonous cyanide compounds. The amounts in pits is tiny, but high doses can be lethal.

EDIBLE SLIME

Slime may be a lot of fun to play with, but there's actually a lot of science behind this stretchy stuff. In fact, when it comes to science, slime can be a a **rule-breaker**. When it's stretched, prodded, and poked it defies expectations. But the best thing about this slime is that it's edible!

You will need

- 10 large marshmallows
- Bowl
- Microwave
- Spatula
- Sieve
- 2 tbsp cornstarch
- 2 tbsp powdered sugar

1 Place your marshmallows in a microwavable bowl. Put them in the microwave on full power for around 10 seconds.

2 Stir the mixture. If it hasn't completely melted, put the bowl back in the microwave for a few more seconds. Repeat until melted.

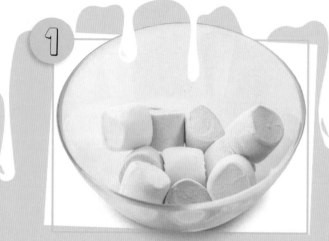

3 Sift a little cornstarch and powdered sugar over the melted marshmallows, stirring as you go. Don't add it all at once or it'll be too difficult to stir.

4 Once you've mixed everything together, your slime should be cool enough to touch and play with—if you can resist eating it first!

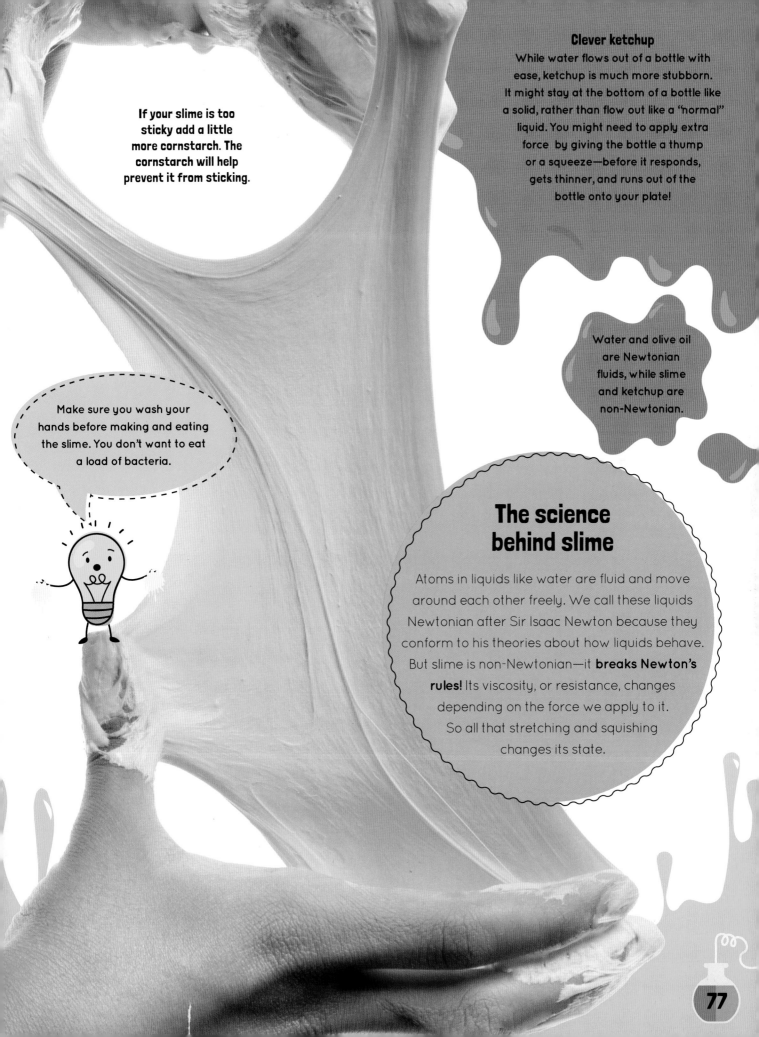

If your slime is too sticky add a little more cornstarch. The cornstarch will help prevent it from sticking.

Clever ketchup
While water flows out of a bottle with ease, ketchup is much more stubborn. It might stay at the bottom of a bottle like a solid, rather than flow out like a "normal" liquid. You might need to apply extra force by giving the bottle a thump or a squeeze—before it responds, gets thinner, and runs out of the bottle onto your plate!

Water and olive oil are Newtonian fluids, while slime and ketchup are non-Newtonian.

Make sure you wash your hands before making and eating the slime. You don't want to eat a load of bacteria.

The science behind slime

Atoms in liquids like water are fluid and move around each other freely. We call these liquids Newtonian after Sir Isaac Newton because they conform to his theories about how liquids behave. But slime is non-Newtonian—it **breaks Newton's rules!** Its viscosity, or resistance, changes depending on the force we apply to it. So all that stretching and squishing changes its state.

DIGESTION: THE JOURNEY

You usually forget about your food once you've eaten it, but that's when the magic of digestion begins! Different parts of your body get to work breaking down complex molecules in food and turning them into simpler molecules **your body can use.** Then all the waste products that your body doesn't need are processed and excreted through your behind.

Enzymes breaking down food

Teeth

Your teeth exert a huge amount of force to tear and crush food. This is called mechanical digestion, and it's about breaking food down into smaller pieces ready for chemical digestion to begin.

Saliva

When saliva mixes with food, the chemical digestion process really kicks off. Saliva contains special things called enzymes which break down fats, lubricate food, and kill bacteria.

Esophagus

All your food and drinks head down this tube that connects your mouth to your stomach.

The digestive tract

Your digestive tract is **one long tube** with a few larger chambers. It runs all the way from your mouth to your behind, and has the combined surface area of a tennis court!

Stomach

Your stomach is a small sack that can expand to hold lots of liquids and solids. Your stomach produces powerful gastric juices that are churned together with food and liquids, then slowly released into your small intestine.

Gastric juices

Stomach

Liver

The liver produces bile, which turns fats and oils into little droplets and makes them easier to digest. The liver also helps to remove toxins from your blood.

Liver

The horrible taste when you're sick comes from the acids and enzymes in your gastric juices. The stomach has to constantly produce a mucus lining so it doesn't get burned by the juices inside it.

Large intestine

This is the last stage of the digestive process where a lot of water is absorbed back into your body, and your gut bacteria break down the fiber in your food. As the bacteria break fiber down, they produce gas. The food then travels down to the rectum—the holding chamber for your poop before you go to the bathroom.

Small intestine

Large intestine

Small intestine

The small intestine is thin but very, very long. It's where a lot more enzymes mix with your food, breaking it down into simpler chemicals which are then absorbed through the walls of the intestine and carried around your body by your bloodstream to the various places they are needed: muscles, skin, bones, brain, eyes—everywhere!

SUPER SALIVA

This is a revolting experiment involving your spit, but it's for scientific purposes: to see the action of **enzymes**. Enzymes are powerhouses that speed up chemical reactions, sometimes by millions of times! Your saliva contains an enzyme called **amylase** that starts breaking down your food, and if you add it to custard it has surprising effects.

Make up the custard according to the instructions and let cool for 15 minutes.

Cornstarch is used as a thickener in many dishes, and can be used to make slime, and something called "oobleck," a fluid that hardens when you stir or hit it.

Divide the custard into the two glasses. Mark these A and B. Spit into glass A about 6-7 times and stir it in, then add a splash of water to glass B and stir it in using a clean spoon.

Set your cutting board on the tray and put something underneath it so it's sitting at an angle. This will be a slide for the custard.

80

What's happening?

Saliva turns the custard watery because the starches that make the custard thick are **sensitive to amylase**. The amylase in your spit speeds up chemical breakdown, and when you compare it to the custard that only had water added, the difference is obvious. That's the effect helpful enzymes can have on food—speeding up reactions so much they sare clear to see.

Instant custard

Saliva

Enzymes

Only instant

This experiment only works with instant custard because it often contains cornstarch. Custard cooked from scratch is made from milk or cream cooked very gently with egg yolk.

The custard with water is still thick and gloopy.

The custard with saliva has turned thin and watery.

4

Take a glass of custard in each hand and pour them down each side of the cutting board at the same time. What happens?

A

B

RUDE FOOD AND EXPLOSIVE PEE

When we swallow food we kick-start a set of amazing processes in our bodies that create **poop, pee, burps, farts, and weird smells**. These are all perfectly natural functions of our digestive process, but many people find them embarrassing or rude so they are rarely talked about. It's a shame, because they are vital to a healthy life, and are packed with fascinating science.

Some foods are fartier than others. Strong smells are usually created by high-protein foods such as meat, fish, lentils, and beans, but the volume of gas is mostly created by high-fiber foods such as grains, root vegetables, onions, cabbage, broccoli, beans, and fruit. The fartiest food on Earth is the Jerusalem artichoke.

Jerusalem artichoke

Fertilizer helps plants grow by adding nutrients to the soil.

Poop

Feces (poop) is the remains of food that hasn't been digested, plus gut bacteria, dead gut lining cells, water, and other waste products the body doesn't need. The brown color comes from **something called bilirubin** and dead blood cells. Poop can be very useful if treated properly: it makes a great fertilizer, can be dried and burned as a fuel, or fermented to produce methane gas.

The standard guide doctors use to identify different types of poop is called the Bristol stool scale.

Farts

Farting is a perfectly natural consequence of a healthy diet: The average adult creates around $2^3/_4$ pints (1.5 liters) of gas every day, and it would cause real problems if we didn't get **rid of it**. Farts are a combination of gases—most of which are created by bacteria in your large intestine—but they also include swallowed air and CO_2. Everyone's farts are different but they are made up of nitrogen, carbon dioxide, hydrogen, and sometimes methane.

The smell of farts comes from tiny amounts of flavor volatiles such as hydrogen sulfide (an eggy smell), trimethylamine (fishy), methyl thiobutyrate (cheesy), and methanethiol (cabbagey).

Farty beans!

Pee

Your digestive system creates a lot of by-products as it breaks down food. Urine is the body's tool for **flushing out by-products** such as urea, creatinine, and uric acid. Your kidneys extract these from your bloodstream alongside excess water, sugars, and other waste substances. Urine also helps to balance your water-to-salt levels.

Asparagus is delicious and has lots of fun physiological effects due to its sulphur and vitamins. These can create a powerful smell in your urine and can even dye it green. Some people enjoy the smell, but others find it unpleasant. A small minority of people claim not to make the smell at all, but it's not clear whether this is true or if they simply aren't able to smell it.

Urine is useful stuff. It's rich in nitrogen so can be used as a fertilizer, and it's also a source of urea which can be used to clear icy paths, cut toxic exhaust emissions in diesel cars, and to produce explosives. In the past, urine was used to make gunpowder.

AMANZING VEGETABLES

Vegetables are nutritional gold. They're full of fiber, vitamins and minerals, and are filling but low in fat and calories—so they're are great for digestion and general health. Modern cooks think of vegetables as being any edible plant other than fruit, nuts, and cereals, but strictly speaking the word refers to **any plant that humans eat**, which leads to some interesting confusions. There are five main types of vegetables.

Roots and tubers

Includes: potatoes, parsnips, carrots, beets, ginger, sweet potatoes, yams

Yam - - - >

These vegetables grow underground and are used by plants as energy stores, so they are usually rich in carbohydrates. They are often easy to store and are important staple foods in countries all around the world.

Flowers and buds

Includes: cauliflower, globe artichokes, capers, zucchini flowers, broccoli

Broccoli - - - >

Look closely at a head of broccoli and you'll see it's made up of tiny bunched flowers. As it matures, the flowers unfurl and turn yellow.

Leaves and salad

Includes: lettuce, spinach, kale, cabbage, watercress, bok choy

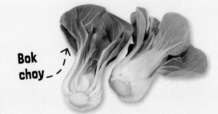

Bok choy - - >

Leaves are eaten less for energy and more for flavor, texture, and as a great source of vitamins, minerals, and dietary fiber.

Potatoes

Zucchini

Broccoli

Carrots

Lettuce

Why do some kids avoid vegetables?

Young people are more sensitive to bitter flavors than adults, and veggies such as cabbage, broccoli, cauliflower and arugula salads are all **slightly bitter**. It's thought to be an evolutionary tool designed to give babies the greatest chance of survival. When we are young we need to put on weight as much as possible so are drawn to sweet and fatty foods. This fades as we get older though, so by the time you're in school, there's no excuse!

Fruit or vegetable?

A lot of foods that we think of as vegetables are, technically speaking, fruit. The definition of a fruit is a "seed-bearing structure grown from flowering plants, made from the ovary after flowering," which is odd because it makes **tomatoes the most popular fruit in the world!** By this definition cucumbers, peppers, chilis, eggplants, olives, bean pods, and even wheat grains are all fruits!

Bulbs and stems

Includes: onion, leeks, asparagus, celery, kohlrabi, garlic

Garlic

Bulbs are fleshy-leafed stems that plants use as energy reserves. Onion bulbs are found underground at the base of the plant, whereas leeks and celery are plant stems.

Podded vegetables

Includes: beans, peas, green beans, soybeans, lentils, okra, peanuts

Peanuts

These are plant seeds, sometimes eaten with the pod (as with green beans) and sometimes on their own. Seeds contain everything needed to create a new plant, including an energy store that we get nutrition from when we eat it.

Onions

Peppers

In 1893 the confusion about tomatoes being fruit or vegetables reached the US Supreme Court, which had to decide on a strict definition to decide how they should be taxed.

Soybeans

Peas

Tomatoes

FANTASTIC FRUIT

Fruit are clever sugary parcels created by plants to **spread their seeds**. Fruit have a delicious sweet-sour taste that tempts animals (including humans) to eat them. The seeds inside fruit are usually covered in a tough coating that remains intact through the digestive system. So when an animal eats a fruit and eventually poops, the seeds are still intact and ready to grow in a new location.

Kiwis

Grapes

Dragonfruit

Lemons

Apples

Lychee

Pineapple

Powerful pineapples

Pineapples contain a very strong enzyme called bromelaine that can be used to **tenderize meat** by breaking down tough fibers until they're soft and juicy. Bromelaine is the reason why some people get a sore mouth when they eat pineapple.

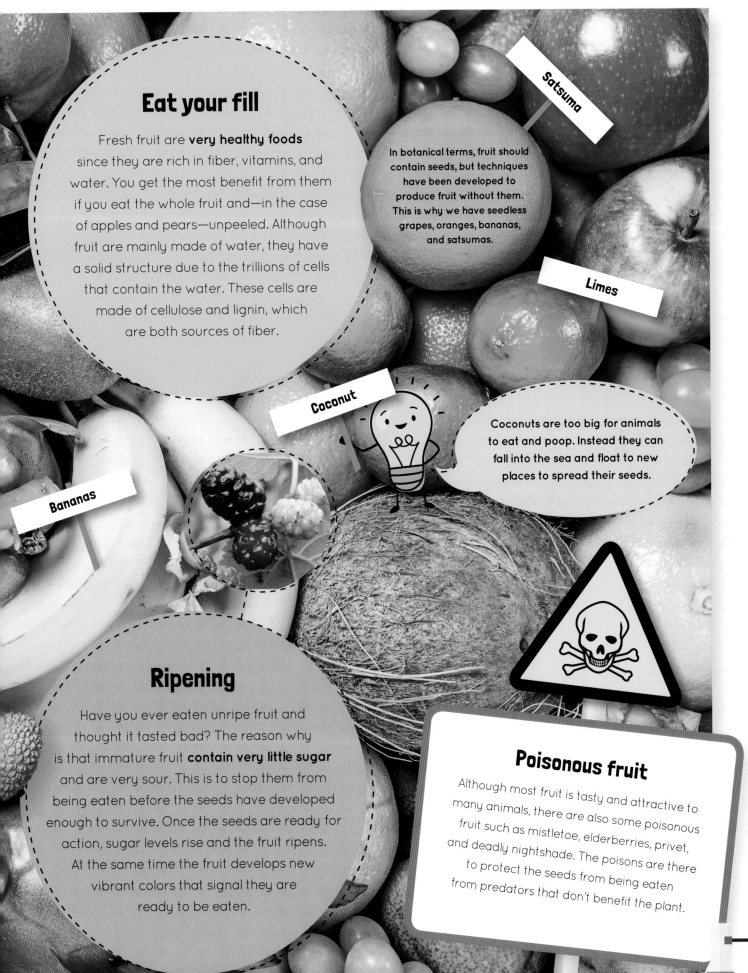

Eat your fill

Fresh fruit are **very healthy foods** since they are rich in fiber, vitamins, and water. You get the most benefit from them if you eat the whole fruit and—in the case of apples and pears—unpeeled. Although fruit are mainly made of water, they have a solid structure due to the trillions of cells that contain the water. These cells are made of cellulose and lignin, which are both sources of fiber.

In botanical terms, fruit should contain seeds, but techniques have been developed to produce fruit without them. This is why we have seedless grapes, oranges, bananas, and satsumas.

Satsuma

Limes

Coconut

Coconuts are too big for animals to eat and poop. Instead they can fall into the sea and float to new places to spread their seeds.

Bananas

Ripening

Have you ever eaten unripe fruit and thought it tasted bad? The reason why is that immature fruit **contain very little sugar** and are very sour. This is to stop them from being eaten before the seeds have developed enough to survive. Once the seeds are ready for action, sugar levels rise and the fruit ripens. At the same time the fruit develops new vibrant colors that signal they are ready to be eaten.

Poisonous fruit

Although most fruit is tasty and attractive to many animals, there are also some poisonous fruit such as mistletoe, elderberries, privet, and deadly nightshade. The poisons are there to protect the seeds from being eaten from predators that don't benefit the plant.

EATING MEAT

Meat is the **flesh of animals**. It's an excellent source of protein, vitamins A and B, and minerals such as iron. Many of us love meat because it has great flavor and is very nutritious. Meat has also had an important cultural and social significance for thousands of years. Humans have eaten meat since prehistoric times, and despite the effort, difficulty, and danger required to get it, meat made up a large proportion of the diet of early humans.

When meat is cooked it takes on a dark brown color. This is due to something called the Maillard reaction.

The makeup of meat

Meat is mostly made of water, protein, and fat. The "red meat" in burgers and steaks comes from animals' muscles, whereas lighter-colored chicken and pork are often called "white meat." **The cost of meat** depends on various things: how ethically the meat has been produced, the type of meat (beef and lamb are more expensive to produce than pork and chicken), and the cut of meat.

Fat

	Expensive	Cheap
Agricultural technique:	Free range and organic	Intensively-farmed
Types of meat:	Beef, lamb, snails	Chicken, pork, insects
Cut of meat:	Fillet, sirloin, breast	Stewing meat, legs

The easier and quicker to cook, the more expensive the cut of meat tends to be. Fillet is the tenderest and easiest cut of beef to cook, and it's also very expensive. Stewing meat takes hours of cooking before it is tender, but is much cheaper.

Muscle fibers

Should we eat meat?

There's no escaping the fact that an animal has to die so we can eat it. And while humans have eaten meat for thousands of years, **we can survive without it**. Despite the nutrition in meat, a plant-based diet can be healthier for some people. Many people object to the killing of animals, and others want to reduce the environmental impact of their diet. People who don't eat meat but eat dairy are called **vegetarians**, and **vegans** avoid all foods made from or by animals.

Types of meat

The most commonly eaten meats are **pork** (from pigs), **beef** (from cows), **poultry** (from birds—mostly chickens), and **lamb** (from sheep). But other meat sources include insects, spiders, and gastropods such as snails. Guinea pig is a very popular feast dish in Peru, and horse is eaten in several countries around the world.

Pork

Spider

Beef

Chicken

Lamb

Horse

Snail

Guinea pig

There's debate about whether fish and seafood are considered meat—but they're definitely animals.

FAKE MEATS

Meat is delicious and an excellent source of protein, but there are many reasons not to eat it. Meat production uses a lot of the world's land, water, and food supply, and creates half of all global greenhouse emissions. And of course, billions of animals have to die to produce it. We can get all the nutrients we need from plants, but many people love the flavor, so **substitutes** have been invented.

Yeast extract

Creating that meaty flavor

It's difficult to recreate that all-important meaty flavor, and it involves a lot of different ingredients. But the nearest vegetable-based flavor ingredient is **yeast extract**. This is often mixed with corn, rice, potato, or wheat starch that's been cooked and broken down, salt, spices, mushroom extracts, MSG (a flavor enhancer), tomato puree, garlic, black pepper, and boiled-down onions, carrots, and celery.

These fluffy soy chunks have very little flavor, so other ingredients are added to make it "meatier."

Heme meat

This is similar in texture and taste to a beef burger, and even cooks like meat. It's made from textured wheat protein, potato protein, and a special blood-like ingredient called **heme** that's grown by genetically-modified yeasts. Coconut oil is added to give the meat juiciness, but interestingly the main ingredient is water.

Textured vegetable protein

Textured vegetable protein is very popular, and also very cheap. It's a by-product left over from **soybeans** after their more valuable oil has been extracted. Soybean flour is heated and pushed through a small opening at high pressure to create an interesting fluffed texture that can absorb a lot of liquid.

Obviously crab sticks do contain meat, but it's worth knowing what's really in them.

Fungus

Some of the best meat substitutes are made by fermenting proteins from a fungus called **fusarium venenatum**. This fungus is dried and mixed with an egg- or potato-based ingredient to bind it together. It's then flavored and processed into various shapes and sizes to create meaty products.

Crab sticks

Crab sticks often aren't made of crab—they're usually made of...fish. Crab is really expensive, so food companies combine a cheap fish called pollock with starch, sugar, egg white, and flavoring, then color it using pink food dye.

Soy and pea protein "chicken"

Several meat substitutes are made using **soy and pea proteins** and fiber. They are cooked with steam, pressure, and cold water to create a chicken-like texture. This is then cut, flavored, and pre-cooked.

Fish protein

Fish-free fish fingers are usually made from **rice flakes** that have been shaped with the help of sodium alginate—an ingredient found in seaweed. The flavor comes from yeast, paprika, salt, and a blend of other natural flavorings.

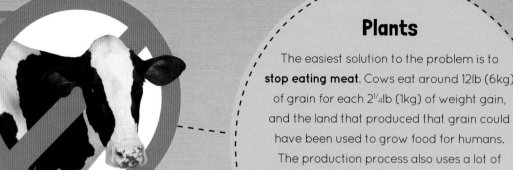

Plants

The easiest solution to the problem is to **stop eating meat**. Cows eat around 12lb (6kg) of grain for each 2¼lb (1kg) of weight gain, and the land that produced that grain could have been used to grow food for humans. The production process also uses a lot of water and energy, and produces a lot of gases that are bad for the environment. So it makes sense for us all to eat a lot less meat, and a lot more plants!

THE FOODS OF THE FUTURE

The world's population is expected to rise from around 7 billion people today, to 9 billion by the year 2040. We need to find new ways to feed everyone from the limited amount of land available. Those extra people will take up more land, use more water, and create more greenhouse gas emissions, too. The good news is there are ingredients we've previously overlooked, and new foods being developed that make **better use of the planet's resources**. The bad news is that you're going to need to be pretty brave to eat some of them!

One solution might be to find more efficient meat sources. Insects are an excellent source of protein that need much less food, water, and land than other meat sources.

Printed food

It's a weird idea and it's mostly been used to create novelty foods so far, but it's not just a gimmick. The advantage of printing food is you can make a meal **exactly as you want it**. So if you have special dietary needs or shop-bought food is too salty, too big, or contains an ingredient you're allergic to, you could create your own version that exactly fits your needs, with minimum waste.

Lab-grown meat

Also known as in vitro ("made in a lab") meat, this is made by taking **meat cells** and feeding them a special liquid so they reproduce. The idea is that they grow and grow until there are enough of them to make an edible burger. In an attempt to give the cells a meat-like structure, they are grown on an edible base that guides the formation of the cells.

GMOs

GMOs (Genetically modified organisms) are living things that have had their **DNA altered**. Many people don't like the idea of editing the genes of food, but the technique can be used to create crops with higher yields, as well as plants that will grow in poor soil. Genetic modification can also be used to help crops grow with less fertilizer, which is good for the planet since fertilizers can be harmful to the environment.

Algae

Algae ranges from tiny single-celled microalgae that grow like a slime in ponds, to giant kelp that float in the sea. If you've ever eaten sushi you'll have eaten a type of algae already: seaweed. Algae is so **efficient** at transforming sunlight into energy through photosynthesis, that algae in the sea are responsible for creating half of the world's oxygen. Farmed algae is grown in huge ponds or glass tanks that allow sunlight to penetrate.

Jellyfish have been popular in parts of China for many years. They are very rubbery, but may make a good diet food in the future since they contain very few calories.

WOULD YOU EAT A BUG?

Perhaps the food of the future has been around for millions of years: insects. They are an amazing food: **eco-friendly, easy to farm, and often very tasty**. In fact, two billion people across the world eat insects as part of their regular diet. In case you're thinking "I'm never going to eat them," you're probably wrong: Almost all flour-based products such as bread, pasta, and noodles contain thousands of tiny fragments of insects. If a crop has been harvested from a field, it's pretty much impossible for it not to contain insect parts!

Cricket flour

Cricket bar

Fried mealworms

Super sustainable

If we eat lots of insects, won't they all die out? Not very likely! There are thought to be up to 50 tons of insects to every human on the planet, and when you collect grasshoppers from a field, it just means that the ones you missed will have access to more food, so they'll reproduce and fill the gap. Insects can also be farmed very efficiently, producing **much more food on much less land** than cows, pigs, or chicken.

The practice of eating insects is called entomophagy.

Honey tastes delicious – but has a strange method of production. It's actually a type of bee vomit!

Why insects are the most eco-friendly meat

Insects grow and reproduce extremely quickly, and they usually eat waste vegetation rather than food that could otherwise have been fed to humans. Unlike cows and sheep, they don't produce a lot of greenhouse gases or need a lot of land. They are, however, small animals so if you're a vegetarian you can't eat them.

Whole locust

New insect-based foods are being invented all the time, from flours and pasta, to baked goods and burgers.

Cricket pasta

What's popular on the insect menu

Crickets
Crickets are so popular in Thailand that 20,000 cricket farms have sprung up to meet demand, and they are also exported across the world. They're mostly fried, but several companies produce cricket protein bars, often covered in chocolate.

Fat-bottomed ants
These are a rare, expensive delicacy from Colombia. Harvested for a few weeks every year, they are soaked in salty water and roasted with salt. The flavor is amazing: a little like smoky bacon, with a salty kick and a crunch.

Mealworms
The larvae of the darkling beetle is one of the most easily available edible insects in Europe. They are easy to farm, with the female laying up to 500 eggs at a time. They have a mushroomy, nutty flavor and make a fantastic Bolognese!

INDEX

Acknowledgments

This book is dedicated to all the amazing teachers, parents, and science communicators across the world who take complex, multi-layered, hard-to-explain science and wrestle it to the ground, break it apart, and then put it back together with a new structure and story (and often an explosion or two) that makes it understandable, exciting, and fun to discover.

Thanks to the entire DK team, especially James Mitchem, for producing such a beautiful project. Also Borra, Louise, and Jan from DML, Andrea Sella, Suzie Sheehy, Brodie Thompson, Eliza Hazlewood and Daisy and Poppy. An extra-huge thank-you to the amazing Georgia Glynn Smith for everything. And lastly, a massive shout out to the audience of my live stage shows who push me every day to come up with new ways to shed light on beautiful, beautiful science. I LOVE you people!

The publisher would like to thank the following for their kind permission to reproduce their photographs:

(Key: a-above; b-below/bottom; c-center; f-far; l-left; r-right; t-top)

2 Dreamstime.com: Anekoho (br); Grafner (crb). 3 Alamy Stock Photo: SureStock (br); Diana Johanna Velasquez (t). 4 Dreamstime.com: William Berry (bl). 5 Dreamstime.com: Dmitry Abaza (crb). 6-7 Dreamstime.com: Orlando Florin Rosu / Orla (c). 8-9 Dreamstime.com: Maglara (Background). 9 Alamy Stock Photo: D. Hurst (bl). 10 123RF.com: Serhiy Kobyakov (tr). Alamy Stock Photo: Science History Images (ca). 15 Dreamstime.com: Irochka (tc); Paulpaladin (ca).

iStockphoto.com: 4kodiak (clb). 16-17 iStockphoto.com: Norasit Kaewsai. 17 123RF.com: Panu Ruangjan / panuruangjan (crb). Dreamstime.com: Shaffandi (br). Fotolia: Eric Isselee (tr). 18 Dorling Kindersley: Stephen Oliver (cla). 19 iStockphoto.com: MarkGillow (crb). 20-21 Dreamstime.com: Mona Makela (b). iStockphoto.com: apodiam (c). 21 Dorling Kindersley: The Body Shop (cb); Stephen Oliver (c). 22-23 iStockphoto.com: ansonsaw. 22 123RF.com: Maggie Molloy / agathabrown (bl). Dreamstime.com: Anna Kucherova / Photomaru (tc). 23 123RF.com: aberration (bl). Alamy Stock Photo: WidStock (clb). Dreamstime.com: Baibaz (cr). 26-27 Dreamstime.com: Winai Tepsuttinun (c). 27 Dreamstime.com: Ckellyphoto (c). Fotolia: He2 (r). 28 123RF.com: Iakov Filimonov (clb). 29 123RF.com: petkov (bl). 30-31 Dreamstime.com: Renzzo (Border). 30 Dreamstime.com: Antoniomaria Iaria (tr). 31 123RF.com: Sucharut Chounyoo (cl); kenmind (tr). Dreamstime.com: Multiart61 (tl). Fotolia: Orkhan Aslanov (cr). 32-33 Dreamstime.com: Okea. 32 Dreamstime.com: Anna Kucherova / Photomaru (crb). 33 Dreamstime.com: Piksel (cra). 34-35 123RF.com: Yuliia Davydenko (b/Background). 36-37 Dreamstime.com: Coffeemill (ca). 37 Dreamstime.com: William Berry (bl); Ra3rn (tc). 38 iStockphoto.com: Coprid (br); Sunnybeach (tr). 39 Alamy Stock Photo: SureStock. Dreamstime.com: Kmiragaya (cl). Getty Images: Howard Berman (tr). iStockphoto.com: Coprid (ca). 40-41 123RF.com: robertsrob (b). 43 Alamy Stock Photo: Martin Shields (l). 44 Dreamstime.com: Ian Andreiev (bl). iStockphoto.com: unpict (cl). 45 Dreamstime.com: Anekoho (br); Grafner (crb). 47 Dreamstime.com: Mona Makela (br); Andrew Buckin / Ka_ru (tc). 48 Alamy Stock Photo: Diana Johanna Velasquez. 50 123RF.com: Sangsak Aeiddam (cl). iStockphoto.com: juliazara (br). 51 Dreamstime.com: Marilyn Gould / Marilyngould (c). 52 123RF.com: Evgeny Karandaev / karandaev (c). Dreamstime.com: Chernetskaya (bl). 56-57 123RF.com: Olena Kaidash. 56 Dreamstime.com: Reamolko (cr). 57 Dreamstime.com: Chernetskaya (cr). 58 Dreamstime.com: Theo Malings (tr). iStockphoto.com: ansonsaw (cr).

62-63 iStockphoto.com: bergamont. 63 Dreamstime.com: Dmitry Abaza (crb); Denismart (tc, cra); Pr2is (tr). 66 Dreamstime.com: Roman Samokhin (cl). 67 Dreamstime.com: Nickjene (r). 68 Dreamstime.com: Bert Folsom / Treb999 (bl). 70-71 123RF.com: Amphaiwan Mahatavon (cb). 71 Photolibrary: FoodCollection (cl). 74 123RF.com: Gamut Pvt Ltd (cr). 75 Dreamstime.com: Nevinates (cl). 81 Alamy Stock Photo: Zoonar GmbH (c). iStockphoto.com: Goldfinch4ever (tc). 82 Dreamstime.com: filmfoto (cl). 84-85 Dreamstime.com: Kurhan (b). 86-87 iStockphoto.com: firina. 88 Dreamstime.com: Dave Bredeson / Cammeraydave (clb). 88-89 123RF.com: dipressionist (Background). 89 Alamy Stock Photo: WENN Rights Ltd (cr). Dreamstime.com: Jakub Gojda (cl); Mexrix (b). 90 123RF.com: Amphaiwan Mahatavon (clb). Dreamstime.com: Anastasiia Skorobogatova (tr). Impossible Foods: (clb/Burger). iStockphoto.com: Nedim_B (crb). 90-91 Dreamstime.com: Stuartbur (b/Fork). 91 123RF.com: Amphaiwan Mahatavon (cb); natika (cla) Dreamstime.com: Fotografieberlin (crb). iStockphoto.com: milanfoto (clb) 92 123RF.com: Eric Isselee / isselee (tc). Dreamstime.com: Tracy Decourcy / Rimglow (cl). Getty Images: Photographer's Choice RF / Jon Boyes. 92-93 123RF.com: dipressionist (Background). 93 Dorling Kindersley: Natural History Museum, London (br). 94 Dreamstime.com: Alle (crb). 95 Alamy Stock Photo: Tim Gainey (l). iStockphoto.com: anamejia18 (cr). 96 Dreamstime.com: Marilyn Gould / Marilyngould (crb).

Cover images: Front: Dreamstime.com: Coffeemill crb

All other images © Dorling Kindersley
For further information see: www.dkimages.com

DK would like to thank:
Sally Beets for editorial assistance, Marie Lorimer for indexing, Sakshi Saluja for picture credits, Anna Wilson for font assistance, and Helene Hilton and Clare Lloyd for helping with photoshoots.

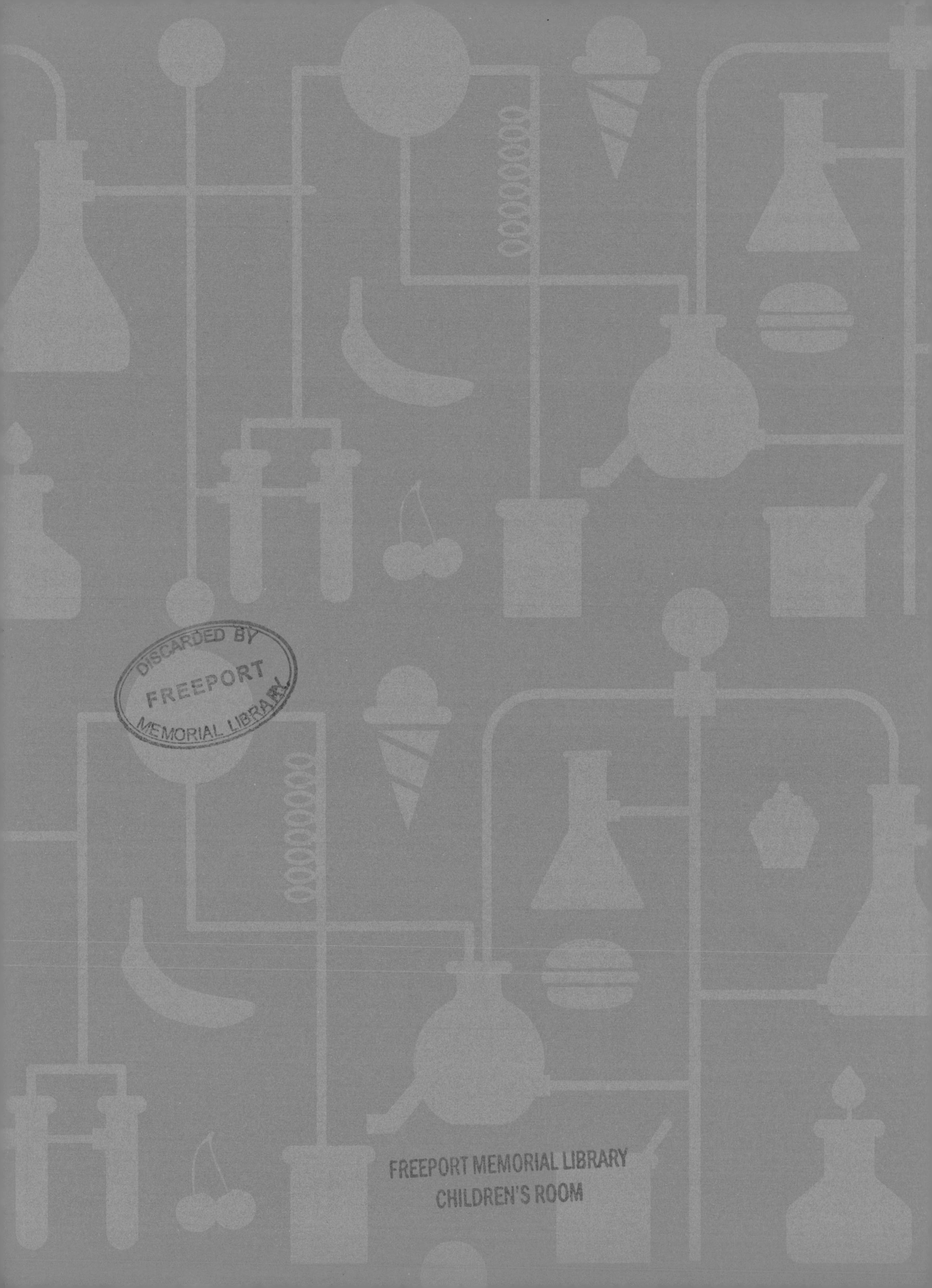